YOU ARE THE CHURCH

The Basics of Biblical Christianity

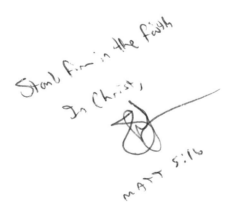

Stand Firm in the faith

In Christ,

MATT 5:16

STEVE LORCH

ISBN-10: 1477625208
EAN-13: 978-1477625200

CONTENTS

PREFACE

To be perfectly honest, I didn't want to write this preface. My editors, however, insisted I do so. I'm a no-nonsense guy and I don't like wasting your time or mine with a lot of fluff. Maybe that comes from working in surgery for 20 years, or maybe that's *why* I've worked in surgery for 20 years. Either way, it's who I am. However, there is wisdom in godly counsel **(Proverbs 15:22)** and my editors felt that you, the reader, would benefit from knowing a bit more about me and about why I wrote this book. So, here you go...

I've taught the Bible since I was 15 years old (I'm 41 as I write this). From the very beginning, I made two simple promises: First, that I would only teach the Bible, verse-by-verse and in context. Second, that I would never bend the Bible to make it say what I wanted it to say or to soften what I did not want it to say. I've never broken those two promises. Through the years, I've come to appreciate that those two simple principles are what make the difference between strong believers and weak ones.

As the founder of Hydromissions International, I travel the world and regularly spend time with Christians from every walk of life. The stories are all the same. Yes, the details are different, but all of us who are truly seeking the Lord are walking on the same narrow path to the same destination. Our struggles are the same as well. We all wish we could be more like Jesus, and we all know that we aren't there yet. My hope is that this book will help bring us all one step closer.

If the Church is to become stronger collectively, we must become stronger individually. I know from my years of teaching that although most of us want to become stronger Christians, we don't always have the tools or the discipline to do so. The whole point of this book is to present those tools in a simple way that makes sense. No big seminary words, no lofty theology – just the Bible, plain and simple. That was actually much harder to pull off than it sounds, and this book took a solid three years to write.

Two last things before we get down to business. First, all scripture quotes in this book are taken from the New American Standard Bible (copyright ©1995 by the Lockman Foundation). I teach from this version because it is accurate. However, the wording and grammar can be a bit odd at times. Second, I use "we" a lot in this book. Not because it was written by a panel of authors (it wasn't), but because I am the Church along with you. I have the same shortcomings and I am subject to the same guiding principles. As a teaching pastor, I have to take my own medicine. I would not expect you to do something that

I am not willing to do myself. Originally, I had titled this book, We Are the Church, but frankly, I didn't write this for me. I wrote it for you. I already know I'm the Church. Hopefully, by the end of this book, you will understand more fully that you are the Church as well.

Steve Lorch
March 30, 2012
Belize City, Belize

INTRODUCTION

Keep it Biblical. Keep it simple. Keep it genuine. In theory, that all sounds great. We've all read mission statements of churches claiming to be "just like the one in the Book of Acts." Yet somehow, genuine Biblical simplicity, at least as it relates to organized Christianity, remains for many an elusive dream.

Jesus teaches, "You shall love the Lord your God with all your heart, and with all your soul, and with all your mind. This is the great and foremost commandment. The second is like it, 'You shall love your neighbor as yourself.' On these two commandments depend the whole Law and the Prophets." **(Matthew 22:37-40)** When it all boils down, there are only two commandments - to love God, and to love people. But how do we do that? And how do we do that *together*?

The early Church faced the same questions, and we learn from their example. **Acts 2:42** tells us "they were continually devoting themselves to the apostles' teaching and to fellowship, to the breaking of bread and to prayer." That is what the early Church did. There were only four basic disciplines to which they devoted themselves: Teaching, Fellowship, Communion, and Prayer. Everything else flowed from those disciplines. They kept it Biblical. They kept it simple. They kept it genuine.

If we are to experience that kind of vibrant spiritual life in our own day, we must be ready to take personal responsibility for our own spiritual growth by living out these four basic disciplines of Bible study, Fellowship, Communion, and Prayer. This applies to each of us as individuals, as families, and as congregations. We are collectively a reflection of what we are individually. We cannot expect our churches to be spiritually strong when we ourselves are content to be spiritually weak. It is time for each of us to step up and be diligent in our own personal walk with Christ. It is time for each of us to look in the mirror, point to ourselves, and say, "This is not a job for the professionals. YOU are the Church!"

CHAPTER 1

BIBLE BASICS, PART 1

Someone once compared the Bible to the ocean – so accessible that a child can wade along its shores, yet so profound that a cargo ship can disappear into its depths. Bible study is a lifelong journey on which we are always learning and maturing in Christ. We never get to the end of it. The next several chapters provide the foundation for that journey as we continue on our own personal walk through the Bible with persistence and accuracy. This material is intended to give us a firm, basic grasp of the Bible, its history and content, how to study it, and most importantly, how to apply it correctly.

Consistent Bible study is a major ingredient to our spiritual growth. Over decades of teaching, we have found that there are only two factors that keep any of us from reading our

Bibles. One is fear, and the other is laziness. Many of us fear that we need to have a seminary degree in order to understand this Book. Still more of us are simply too lazy to take the time to read it for ourselves. We would rather read a book *about* the Bible than read the actual Bible. The following chapters remove the fear factor and show us that the Bible truly is accessible to anyone willing to take the time to read it. Sadly, we can do nothing about the laziness. That remains entirely up to the individual, ourselves included.

We are incredibly blessed to live in a time in which we have so many excellent, reliable resources to give us insight into original Bible languages, history, and culture. Throughout these chapters, we will highlight some of the ones that have been particularly helpful over the years and we will explain how to use them effectively. We will also demonstrate several methods and tips that can breathe new life into our personal and group Bible study.

Along the way, we will develop a framework for consistent theological thinking by explaining some key principles for studying Scripture as a unified whole. Such an approach allows us to deal with difficult or seemingly contradictory passages in a way that preserves the truth for what it is, while not avoiding the tough stuff. We end up with a balanced, comprehensive view of God's Word that gives us a firm spiritual footing. "As a result, we are no longer to be children, tossed here and there by waves and carried about by every wind of doctrine, by the trickery of men, by craftiness in deceitful scheming; but speaking the truth in love, we are to grow up in all aspects into Him who is the head, even Christ…" **(Ephesians 4:14-15)**

By the end, we will be much better equipped to teach and/or participate in group Bible study together. Timothy was encouraged "to give attention to the public reading of Scripture, to exhortation and teaching." **(1 Timothy 4:13)** Paul wrote, to "take pains with these things; be absorbed in them, so that your progress will be evident to all. Pay close attention to yourself and to your teaching; persevere in these things, for as you do this you will ensure salvation both for yourself and for those who hear you." **(1 Timothy 4:15-16)**

We can think of no better way to optimize the Church experience than to spark our interest in understanding the Bible in such a way that it effectively speaks into our lives and into the lives of others. A firm foundation in Scripture is essential for every believer both individually and corporately. Our willingness to share truth with each other from God's Word plays a vital role in "the equipping of the saints for the work of service, to the building up of the body of Christ…" **(Ephesians 4:12)**

Before we go any further, there are a few basic principles that should be made clear. First, we are not expected to know everything about the Bible. However, we are expected to apply what we do know. We should be more concerned about our application than we are about our education. Jesus said, "If anyone loves Me, he will keep My word; and My Father will love him, and We will come to him and make Our abode with him." **(John 14:23)** As far as knowing His Word is concerned, we can be confident that He has given us a Helper. In the same passage, Jesus assures us that, "the Helper, the Holy Spirit, whom the Father will send in My name, He will teach you all things, and bring to your remembrance all that I said to you." **(John 14:26)**

Second, we will get out of our Bible study only what we put into it. Disciplined exercise is as necessary for spiritual fitness as it is for physical fitness, "for bodily discipline is only of little profit, but godliness is profitable for all things, since it holds promise for the present life and also for the life to come." **(1 Timothy 4:8)**

Third, we study the Word of God to better know the God of the Word. The Bible is not an end unto itself. We would do well to remember that "we all have knowledge. Knowledge makes arrogant, but love edifies. If anyone supposes that he knows anything, he has not yet known as he ought to know; but if anyone loves God, he is known by Him." **(1 Corinthians 8:1-3)** When speaking to the religious leaders of the day, Jesus rebuked them saying, "You search the Scriptures because you think that in them you have eternal life; it is these that testify about Me; and you are unwilling to come to Me so that you may have life." **(John 5:39-40)** Let us take these passages as a solemn reminder against filling our heads while neglecting our hearts.

A Brief History of the Bible.

Before we discuss the practice of Biblical Christianity, we have to discuss the Bible itself. We must be confident that the Bible is a reliable, credible source before we bet our lives on it. For starters, what is the Bible, how were its contents determined, and how was it preserved? Before we answer these questions, we must make a very important distinction between Bible "preservation" and Bible "translation."

Preservation strictly deals with how the original text (in its original Hebrew, Aramaic, and Greek) was accurately kept intact from the time it was first penned by the author until now. A modern example of preservation would be a photocopy. It copies exactly what it sees without any interpretation. This chapter addresses issues of preservation.

Translation, on the other hand, strictly deals with how the words and ideas from the original text came to be written in our own languages of today. A modern example of translation would be speaking through an interpreter. He/she must first determine the intended meaning of the original words of the speaker before converting them into the language of the listener. The next chapter addresses issues of translation.

The reason why it is so important for us to distinguish between preservation and translation is because the great majority of those who argue against the Bible will say incorrectly that their skepticism has to do with issues of preservation ("It was written so long ago and has changed so much. How can we possibly know what it really says?" etc.). In fact, their problem lies squarely in the realm of translation. We know exactly what the words of the Bible *say*, we just don't like what those words *mean*. And that is a VERY big difference!

What is the Bible? The word "Bible" (biblos/Byblos) literally refers to a roll of papyrus, an early form of paper made from strips of a plant that grew along the Nile River. Paper was very expensive, and as such, it was used to document only the most important information (laws, government records, sacred writings, etc.). Over time, the term came to refer to the collection of Scriptures written on such paper.

The Bible was written over a period of 1500 years (1400 BC- 95 AD) by about 40 different men. It contains 66 books called the 'canon' (Greek for 'rule' or 'measuring line'). The Bible is divided into the Old & New Testaments ('testament' simply means 'will' or 'covenant'). There are 39 books in the Old Testament (Genesis thru Malachi), and 27 books in the New Testament (Matthew thru Revelation). This literary collection includes history, poetry, allegory, prophecy, theology and just about every kind of writing in between. From a purely secular perspective, there is no other literary work in all of history that compares to the sheer magnitude and scope of this extraordinary Book. All religion aside, everyone, especially those who consider themselves educated, should read the Bible at least once simply for its literary merit alone.

As for its purpose, the Bible is the written account of God's personal dealing with mankind. It is a love letter, our handbook for living, and the owner's manual for the human soul. It contains all of the necessary direction we need for every situation we may face in this life. Where there is no direct statement made for a particular situation, there are definite principles in the Bible that can be applied to it. Here is the great conflict over the Bible: The fact that this Book actually makes a claim upon our lives is the central issue for those who do not want any part of it. As believers, our challenge is to understand that as we look for answers and direction in this life, we need to look no further than what God has already written in His Word.

As for its focus, the Bible consistently points us to the person of Jesus. This can be summarized as follows: In the Old Testament, Jesus is predicted; in the Gospels, Jesus is revealed; in the Acts, Jesus is preached; in the Epistles, Jesus is explained; and in the Revelation, Jesus is expected. The theme of the Messiah that runs throughout Scripture is unavoidable.

Every believer in history looks to the Christ. Old Testament believers looked to His coming and all of us look to His return.

As for its authority, God says what He means and He means what He says. God will not contradict His written Word. Truth is not subjective. Truth is truth because it is true. God is the final authority concerning our theology and our actions. Not to believe the Bible is one thing – that is a matter of personal opinion – but to say that something is in the Bible when it is not, or to say that something is not in the Bible when it is, is the very definition of heresy. The clarity of the Bible is most often blurred simply because we do not take the time to read it for ourselves. If any person, no matter how scholarly or well educated, has not actually read the Bible cover to cover for themselves, he/she has no right or credibility to comment on its content or on its application. For our own part, we must exercise our own due diligence in verifying anyone's claims about the Bible. We must be like the Bereans who "received the word with great eagerness, examining the Scriptures daily to see whether these things were so." **(Acts 17:11)**

How were the contents of the Bible determined? There are countless volumes written on this subject for those who want to study it further. Here, we are simply presenting a brief overview of how the Bible came to be. This topic has always been controversial. When faced with a debate on the subject, we should be careful not to get bogged down in the multitude of tangents that inevitably arise. Some questions are sincere and deserve sincere answers, but we must also beware of those who have "a morbid interest in controversial questions and disputes about words, out of which arise envy, strife, abusive language, evil suspicions, and constant friction between men of depraved mind and deprived of the truth." **(I Timothy 6:4-5)**

We start with the general criteria for a book's "canonicity" (again, "canon" simply means "rule" or "measuring line", and it refers to the 66 books that complete our Bible today). Please note that if we were actually trying to prove a book's validity here in this section, the following examples would be considered circular reasoning because we are quoting from the very books that we would be trying to prove. However, we are not in the process of validating books here. We are simply showing the criteria by which they were validated.

In determining whether or not a book made it into the Bible, the book had to be...

1. **Authoritative.** Does it claim to be of God? If so, then it inherently makes a claim upon our life. Again, here is the true battle over the Book. We cannot *prove* that the Bible is the Word of God. This has always been, and always will be a matter of personal faith. Many of us want proof beyond the shadow of a doubt that God wrote the Bible. We even want His signature and a handwriting analysis! But this leaves no room for faith, does it? And that is precisely why God will not allow some things to be proven in that way. "Now faith is the assurance of things hoped for, the conviction of things not seen. For by it the men of old gained approval... and without faith it is impossible to please Him, for he who comes to God must believe that He is and that He is a rewarder of those who seek Him." **(Hebrews 11:1,2,6)** We must become very comfortable with the fact of

faith, acknowledging without excuse and without falsehood where the hard facts end and where faith begins. This is simply being honest. And honesty matters – we cannot pursue truth without it.

2. **Prophetic.** Is the writer considered a spokesperson for God? We've been given very clear instruction about our acceptance of those claiming to be prophets. In the Old Testament, God said, "…the prophet who speaks a word presumptuously in My name which I have not commanded him to speak, or which he speaks in the name of other gods, that prophet shall die. You may say in your heart, 'How will we know the word which the LORD has not spoken?' When a prophet speaks in the name of the LORD, if the thing does not come about or come true, that is the thing which the LORD has not spoken. The prophet has spoken it presumptuously; you shall not be afraid of him." (**Deuteronomy 18:20-22**) The New Testament tells us, "…that no prophecy of Scripture is a matter of one's own interpretation, for no prophecy was ever made by an act of human will, but men moved by the Holy Spirit spoke from God." (**2 Peter 1:20-21**) We are instructed to "…not believe every spirit, but (to) test the spirits to see whether they are from God, because many false prophets have gone out into the world. By this you know the Spirit of God: every spirit that confesses that Jesus Christ has come in the flesh is from God; and every spirit that does not confess Jesus is not from God; this is the spirit of the antichrist, of which

you have heard that it is coming, and now it is already in the world." **(1 John 4:1-3)**

3. **Authentic.** Does it tell the truth? Truth is objective. We do follow certain guidelines to determine what is true. We start with one simple question: Are there any contradictions internally within an individual book itself, or externally between an individual book and the other books of the Bible? The answer often weeds out many of the supposed "lost books" of the Bible that make their way into the media from time to time.

4. **Dynamic.** Does it have life-changing power? We only know this after the fact, when we see the lives that have been changed by it.

5. **Received.** Has it been accepted by God's people (those for whom it was written)? This speaks to the classic argument that "a group of men got together to pick and choose which books to put in the Bible." More accurately, the various councils (Jamnia, Carthage, etc.) merely affirmed as Scripture those books that were *already* accepted by God's people.

Now that we have a general idea of the basic criteria, we can look at some of the more specific things that determined whether or not a book made it into the Bible.

The Old Testament. In order for a book to be included in the Old Testament it had to be written either by Moses or by another one of the prophets. The first five books of the Bible were written by Moses. These books are called the "Pentateuch" ("penta" meaning "five"), and are often referred to as "The Law." The remaining books of the Old Testament are often referred to as "The Prophets." When the New Testament uses the term "the Law and the Prophets" **(Matthew 22:40, Luke 16:16, Acts 13:15, Romans 3:21, etc.)** it is referring to the entire Old Testament as we know it.

There is significant evidence that the books of the Old Testament were most likely compiled and finalized by Ezra, Nehemiah, and a council of Jews known as the "Great Synagogue" around 400 BC. According to the Babylonian Talmud (a 3rd century book about Jewish law and ethics), the Jews believed that after Malachi (around 400 BC), the Holy Spirit departed from Israel, therefore ending God's revelation through Old Testament Scripture.

Old Testament books fell into 4 categories of acceptance:

1. **Accepted by all.**

2. **Questioned by some.**

3. **Rejected by all.**

4. **Apocryphal (non-biblical; accepted by some).** Catholic Bibles contain a section called "The Apocrypha." This includes several books that describe the Intertestamental period (the time between the Old and New Testaments from around 400 BC to around 30 AD). There are many reasons for these books not to be included in our Bibles. The most significant is the fact that none of these books were accepted as Scripture by the Jews themselves.

Once again, there are entire volumes written on this subject for those who want to study it further.

Of the 39 books in our Old Testament, 34 were accepted by all. Only 5 were questioned by some. These were: **The Song of Solomon** (originally considered too sensual), **Ecclesiastes** (originally considered too skeptical), **Esther** (God's name is never mentioned), **Ezekiel** (originally thought to contradict Mosaic law), and **Proverbs** (originally thought to contradict itself).

The Old Testament was written in Hebrew with some Aramaic (**Ezra 4:8 to 6:18; Ezra 7:12-26; Jeremiah 10:11; and Daniel 2:4b to 7:28**). Closely related to Hebrew, the Jews picked up some Aramaic while exiled in Babylon. The words and customs in the Old Testament support that each book was written exactly when it claims to have been written. For example, if a book claims to have been written in 1835 but states that it was first sent to the publisher via e-mail from a fast food restaurant, we would rightly conclude that the book was not written in 1835 (the fast food culture didn't begin until the 1930's, and the first e-mail wasn't sent until the early 1970's).

All but 9 Old Testament books (**Ruth, Judges, Song of Solomon, Ecclesiastes, Esther, Ezra, Nehemiah, 1** and **2 Chronicles**) are directly quoted in the New Testament. Jesus Himself quoted at least 36 Old Testament passages from 13 different Old Testament books. He also made reference to many others.

The New Testament. In order for a book to be included in the New Testament it had to be written either directly by, or with the authority of an apostle directly under the authority of Christ. The only books in the New Testament not written directly by an apostle are: **Mark** (Mark was Peter's scribe), **Luke/Acts** (Luke was Paul's traveling companion), **James & Jude** (both were brothers of Jesus, and both met the criteria for an apostle as given in **Acts 1:21-22**), and possibly **Hebrews** (thought by many to be written by Paul or by a close associate).

The New Testament was written in common Greek, the language of the ordinary people. As with the Old Testament, we find that the words and customs in the New Testament support that each book was written exactly when it claims to have been written.

In terms of consistency, truth from the New Testament is foreshadowed in the Old, while truth from the Old Testament is revealed and fulfilled in the New. There is a classic saying that, "the New is in the Old concealed; the Old is in the New revealed." There are many believers today who claim that because we are living in "New Testament times," there is no need for us to bother with the Old Testament. In fact, just the opposite is true. When we understand the Old Testament, we have a much deeper understanding of what the New Testament fulfills. The two go hand in hand, and both are vital to our spiritual growth and understanding.

How was the Bible Preserved? We do not have any of the original Bible manuscripts. We have no physical samples of the actual handwriting of God, of Moses, of Paul, or of any of the other Biblical writers. What we do have are extremely accurate copies of copies of copies. The first mechanically printed Hebrew Old Testament was made in 1488, followed by the printed Greek New Testament in 1516. Before then, all copies of Scripture were done meticulously by hand.

The Old Testament. Genesis through Deuteronomy were written by Moses around 1400 BC. The book of Job is considered to be the oldest book in the Bible, written close to the time of Abraham (around 1900 BC). Before that time, the Bible narrative was passed down orally. According to Scripture, Adam himself lived until Lamech (Noah's father) was 56 years old. **(Genesis 5)** Noah himself lived until Abraham was 60 years old. **(Genesis 10)** In other words, Adam could have sat down and talked first-hand with his great-great-great-great-great-great-great grandson about what it was really like to live in the Garden of Eden. The oral record becomes much more reliable when we consider that the personal eyewitnesses could have given the accounts directly to several generations at once.

After the oral record, professional scribes (record keepers) are referenced as early as **2 Samuel** (around 930 BC), and each king of Israel, beginning with Saul (around 1095 BC), was required to write an entire copy of the law when he first took office. **(Deuteronomy 17:18)**

Until 600 AD, the Hebrew Old Testament did not contain any vowel points, punctuation, or spaces between words. These upgrades originated with a group called the Masoretes (meaning 'tradition') who set down rules for copying Scripture. These dedicated men took detail to a whole new level. They counted everything that could be counted, and standardized everything that could be standardized. They measured the size of the pages, the columns, the spaces between words and letters. Even the color of the ink and the clothing to be worn by the scribes were regulated.

Each manuscript was submitted for rigorous inspection and quality control. No alterations were allowed. If the scribe had any suggested corrections, they had to be written in the margins. If the manuscript was found to be in error in any way, it was burned and the scribe would have to start all over again from the very beginning (remember, this was all done by hand). When a new scroll finally did pass inspection, the older one was destroyed to prevent poor quality copies from being circulated. A tedious and thankless job for sure, but we owe a lot to the Masoretes.

A major development in Bible preservation came with the discovery of the Dead Sea Scrolls in Qumran in 1947. These 900 documents include material from every Old Testament book except for **Esther** and **Nehemiah**. The oldest of these manuscripts is a copy of the book of **Isaiah**, and is dated to 100 BC. Written on leather parchment, sealed in clay jars, and hidden in caves, these documents are amazingly well preserved. Some of them, along with reproductions, are on display at the Shrine of the Book in Jerusalem. They can also be viewed online at http://dss.collections.imj.org.il.

The New Testament: Although the New Testament was not copied with as many quality control measures as the Old Testament, there are other factors that help to confirm the accuracy and credibility of the text.

First, we have age proximity. The New Testament manuscripts that we do possess are very close in time to the original manuscripts, and are therefore more likely to be accurate. The entire New Testament was completed in the lifetime of the apostles, ending with the death of John (around 100 AD). The earliest known New Testament manuscript is a tiny fragment of the **Gospel of John**, dating to 125 AD, a mere 25 years after the author's lifetime.

Second, and perhaps more importantly, we have volume. There are literally thousands (5,300+) of preserved, ancient Greek New Testament manuscripts that we can compare to each other to determine the wording and content of the original. For example:

> Manuscript #1: Jesus Christ is the Son of Gd.
> Manuscript #2: Christ Jesus is the Son of God.
> Manuscript #3: Jesus Christ s the Son of God.
> Manuscript #4: Jesus Christ is th Son of God.
> Manuscript #5: Jsus Christ is the Son of God.

As our example shows, variants do exist among some of the manuscripts. However, most of the variations are differences in spelling or word order, and this is not nearly as critical as we might think.

Aoccdrnig to rscheearch at an Elingsh uinervtisy, it deosn't mttaer in waht oredr the ltteers in a wrod are, olny taht the frist and lsat ltteres are at the rghit pcleas. The rset can be a toatl mses and you can sitll raed it wouthit a porbelm. Tihs is bcuseae we do not raed ervey lteter by ilstef, but the wrod as a wlohe.

For the sake of transparency, a good study Bible will include any variations in the margin. We can also say with great confidence that none of our fundamental Christian doctrines are based upon a verse that has any textual variations.

So, why should we study the Bible? For starters, it's all good. Every word in the Bible is there for a reason. "All Scripture is inspired by God and profitable for teaching, for reproof, for correction, for training in righteousness; that the man of God may be adequate, equipped for every good work." **(2 Timothy 3:16-17)** There is both safety and challenge in reading through the Bible. The safety comes in knowing that we are standing on solid ground (God wrote it). The challenge comes in covering every topic as God wants it to be covered (we have to deal with issues that we would rather avoid).

There have always been and always will be new false teachers and teachings. When we are familiar with the real thing, what it says and what it does not say, we can spot any counterfeit that comes along. However, familiarity only comes from spending time in the actual Bible. Though sometimes helpful, books and study guides about the Bible are no substitute for spending consistent time in the actual, genuine Word of God.

God's Word gets to the heart like nothing else can. "For the Word of God is living and active and sharper than any two-edged sword, and piercing as far as the division of soul and spirit, of both joints and marrow, and able to judge the thoughts and intentions of the heart." **(Hebrews 4:12)** None of us are very good at "judging the thoughts and intentions of the heart." In fact, we are not even capable of understanding our own heart! "The heart is more deceitful than all else and is desperately sick; Who can understand it?" **(Jeremiah 17:9)** Well, the Word of God can (and does) understand the heart, even down to the "division of soul and spirit." When we read Scripture – real Scripture - it changes us. It forces us to confront ourselves, our motives, and our actions. There is no other book that performs this spiritual surgery with such perfect skill and consistency.

The Bible always works. Lives are effectively changed through God's Word. "For as the rain and the snow come down from heaven, and do not return there without watering the earth, and making it bear and sprout, and furnishing seed to the sower and bread to the eater; so shall My word be which goes forth from My mouth; it shall not return to Me empty, without accomplishing what I desire, and without succeeding in the matter for which I sent it." **(Isaiah 55:10-11)**

The fact that God Himself is the One who will make His Word effective is one of the greatest promises on which a Bible teacher can rest. This promise stands regardless of our degree of ability, creativity, or eloquence. This promise stands whether or not we have any new insights, illustrations, or anything clever to say. This promise stands whether or not we have church programs, a nice building, or the latest strategy for evangelism. If we simply will commit to reading the Word of God personally and within our churches, it WILL have results. For He Himself has promised it! This promise stands simply because He makes it stand.

CHAPTER 2

BIBLE BASICS, PART 2

Bible translation is difficult. It requires many dedicated, talented lives and countless resources. The privilege of reading God's Word in our mother tongue is not one that is shared by everyone. At the time of this writing, there are over 6,900 languages in the world. Only 2,400 have their own written Bible, and most of these are only partial with just a few books translated. In this chapter we will discuss how the original Hebrew, Aramaic, and Greek came to be written in our modern languages of today.

When we talk about Bible translation, we have to start with the nature of the Bible itself. We believe that the Scriptures came to us as "...men moved by the Holy Spirit spoke from God."**(2 Peter 1:21)**. As such, two basic principles apply:

1. **Eternal Relevance**. Because the Bible is God's Word, it speaks to everyone, in every age, in every culture. God is eternal (past, present, and future). Likewise, His Word is eternal. The Bible contains timeless, universal truths that apply to all of us regardless of gender, race, age, socioeconomic status, or anything else that might otherwise divide us. "For (we) are all sons of God through faith in Christ Jesus. For all of (us) who were baptized into Christ have clothed (ourselves) with Christ. There is neither Jew nor Greek, there is neither slave nor free man, there is neither male nor female; for (we) are all one in Christ Jesus." **(Galatians 3:26-28)** None of us would study the Bible if we did not believe that it held some relevance to our present life.

2. **Historical Peculiarity.** Because the Bible was written in human words in history, it bears the flavor of the original language, time, and culture in which it was written. For the most part, the Bible is set within a Middle-eastern, agricultural society that pre-dates much of what we are familiar with today. For many of us, the difference is as great as moving from a big city out to a farm in the middle of nowhere. There are many practical, historical, and cultural references to a way of life that most of us will only learn about second-hand. A few books that are especially helpful in understanding the historical peculiarities of the Bible are

the "**Zondervan Pictoral Encyclopedia of the Bible**" (5 volumes, ISBN 0-310-33188-9), **"Nelson's New Illustrated Bible Dictionary"** (ISBN 0-8407-2071-8), and **"Nelson's Illustrated Manners and Customs of the Bible"** (ISBN 07852-5042-5).

Before we can rightly apply the Bible to our own lives, we must be sure of what it actually says. We must be equally sure of what it does not say. This is where "context" and "content" become extremely important. If we view Scripture as a painting, the context would include the canvas, the frame, the paint, the brush, and the painter. The content, on the other hand, would be the actual scene that is depicted. All of these elements are necessary, and each must be in its proper place for us to fully understand and appreciate the work for what it is.

The term for studying the Bible's context and content is called "exegesis." We are trying to discover the original, intended meaning to those who first received it. In other words, "What did it mean to *them, then?*"

We start by asking questions. Specifically, who, what, when, where, and (our favorite) why? When asking questions of context, there are two main branches to consider:

1. **Historical Context**. Historical context attempts to put the reader back into the time and place of the original writing. We are trying to find out more about the timing, culture, politics, geography, technology, etc., of the day. Jerusalem, for example, was a much different place under Solomon's prosperous reign than it was during Hezekiah's day when the Assyrian army was attacking

the city. The author, the audience, and the purpose of the writing are also important. For example, we would expect a public speech given to calm down an angry crowd to be very different from a private letter written to encourage a close friend. Most study Bibles and commentaries give a general overview of historical context at the beginning of each book.

2. **Literary Context**. Literary context looks at how words relate to each other in a sentence, and how sentences relate to each other in a paragraph. This is what we typically mean when we say that something has been "taken out of context." A helpful tip for keeping verses in context is the 20/20 rule: When studying a specific verse, read the 20 verses before it and the 20 verses after it to see how everything fits together.

When asking questions of content, there are also two main branches to consider:

1. **Words**. Since words change over time, we want to know the actual, original meaning of the word in its original language. Anyone who speaks a second language knows that there are subtleties and nuances in the words and phrases that are very hard to explain in another language. They simply do not translate well. For those of us not fluent in the Biblical languages, we highly recommend the following reference books: The **"Complete Word Study Dictionary, Old Testament"** (ISBN 0-89957-667-2), and the **"Complete Word Study Dictionary, New Testament"** (ISBN 0-89957-663-X).

2. **Grammar**. Since words have meaning within sentences, we want to know the structural details of those sentences. For example, to whom or to what does the word refer? Is it a statement, question, or command? Consider the possibilities in the sentence, **"you shut the door"** (remember, ancient Hebrew had no punctuation). This can be translated several ways, depending on the context:

"You shut the door." A statement that you did, in fact, shut the door. However, is the "you" singular or plural?

"You shut the door?" A question that could be asking if you did, in fact, shut the door; or it could be asking an implied question about the reason why you might have done such a thing. The first is a simple, direct question, but the second is a complex, indirect question that is concerned with the motives and consequences of the action.

"You! Shut the door!" A bold command, urgently demanding that you (singular or plural) should go and shut the door immediately.

The lesson to be learned is that the context will almost always clarify the content.

Ultimately, we want to end up at application. James tells us to "prove (ourselves) doers of the word, and not merely hearers who delude (ourselves)." **(James 1:22)** The term for applying Biblical truth to our own lives is called "hermeneutics." Essentially, we are trying to find the present-day relevance in the ancient texts. In other words, "What does it mean to *us, now*?"

Proper application (hermeneutics) is dependent upon proper interpretation (exegesis). A passage will not mean what it never meant. If we misinterpret the context, we will misinterpret the content, and we will ultimately misinterpret the application.

Most false doctrine comes from attempting to apply Scripture to our lives without fully understanding or accepting what that Scripture truly says in its proper context. Since we all have our own ideas of what we would like the Bible to say, we must be all the more careful not to superimpose those ideas onto God's Word. Solid, Biblical investigation builds a solid, Biblical foundation for solid, Biblical application. There are no shortcuts.

The fact that language and culture are in constant change makes it necessary for ongoing Bible translation. It makes no sense for any of us to own a Bible that we cannot read and understand. However, many factors go into publishing a new Bible translation (things are not as simple as modernizing the text into the new language or culture). The fact that we are reading the Bible in our own language means that we have already been subjected to someone's interpretation. We must choose wisely! This section gives us a partial overview of some of the difficult choices that Bible translators face as they try to keep God's Word accurate, alive, and relevant.

Textual Choices. Which ancient manuscripts will be used as the basis for the new translation? We have thousands of manuscripts with varying degrees of accessibility (not everyone can just walk in and study the Dead Sea Scrolls). Translators want to be sure that the Hebrew, Aramaic, or Greek text being used is as close as possible to the original as when it left the author's hand. This may seem like an obvious point until we realize that many publications claiming to be Bible "translations" are actually using a modern Bible as their base text. In those cases, what we are seeing are translations *of* translations, which are inherently less accurate than those that stay closer to the original source.

Linguistic Choices. Does the translation focus more on the actual words, or on the intended thoughts behind those words? Linguistic choices involve three key elements: The original language (what we are translating <u>from</u> - Hebrew, Aramaic or Greek), the receptor language (what we are translating <u>to</u> - English, Spanish, etc.), and the historical distance (the gap between the original language and the receptor language, including things like words, grammar, idioms, cultural references, etc.).

There are three basic approaches to linguistic choices:

1. **Literal**. A "word-for-word" approach. This attempts to stay very close to the original words and grammar. A literal translation is best for it's accuracy, but can sometimes be awkward to read.

2. **Dynamic**. A "functional" approach. This attempts to keep the meaning of the original while saying it in a way that we would normally say it today. A dynamic translation is the middle-of-the-road. It is fairly easy to read and keeps fairly close to the original word meanings. However, it can also take significant liberties with interpretation in some areas.

3. **Paraphrase**. A "free" approach. This attempts to translate the major ideas of the original with less concern for the exact words. A paraphrase is not a true translation. It is more like a running commentary. Many paraphrases are the work of a single author and, depending

on the passage, they tend either to be right on target or way off the mark with very little in between.

The following chart shows some of the most common translations in terms of literal, dynamic, or paraphrase:

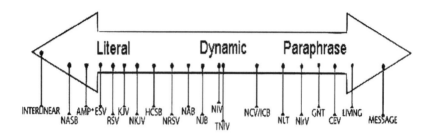

In addition to textual and linguistic choices, there are some problem areas deserving special attention. Consider the following:

Weights, Measures, and Money. Are we talking about specific units or about general amounts? One of the best examples is that of the "denarius" (a Roman silver coin). One aspect of the coin (its value) is illustrated in **Luke 7:41-42** when Jesus says, "A moneylender had two debtors: one owed five hundred denarii, and the other fifty. When they were unable to repay, he graciously forgave them both. So which of them will love him more?" In this context, Jesus is referring to the fact that both people owed very large amounts of money that neither could repay (in Biblical times, a denarius was worth about a day's wage). Another aspect of the coin (its specific design) is illustrated in **Luke 20:21-25** when "they questioned (Jesus), saying, 'Teacher, we know that You speak and teach correctly, and You are not partial to any, but teach the way of God in truth. Is it lawful for us to pay taxes to Caesar, or not?' But He detected their trickery and said to them, 'Show Me a _denarius_. Whose likeness and inscription does it have?' They said, 'Caesar's.' And He said to them, 'Then render to Caesar the things that are Caesar's, and to God the things that are God's.'" In this context, Jesus is addressing the issue of rightful ownership by pointing out the image of Caesar that was printed on the actual coin itself. His illustration would not have worked with other types of coins that did not bear the face of the Roman emperor, nor would it have worked if He had just said, "Show me a day's wage" without specifying the denomination. This is why we leave the unit as "denarius" without further interpretation.

Euphemisms. These are nice ways of saying uncomfortable things. The Bible often uses euphemisms, especially in reference to bodily functions. For instance, in **Genesis 31:34-35**, we read, "Now Rachel had taken the household idols and put them in the camel's saddle, and she sat on them. And Laban felt through all the tent but did not find them. She said to her father, 'Let not my lord be angry that I cannot rise before you, for _the manner of women_ is upon me.' So he searched but did not find the household idols." Laban did not make Rachel get up because she was telling him that she was in the middle of her menstrual cycle.

Vocabulary. Every language has words that do not have equivalents. Sometimes we end up using the definition of the word rather than just the word itself. A good example is "love". English has the one word, but Biblical Greek has three: "eros" (passionate love), "philia" (brotherly/friendship love), and "agape" (unconditional/familial love).

Wordplays. These are words with similar spellings or sounds but with different meanings. Wordplays are often used in Biblical names, especially when those names are changed for a specific reason. Take for example **Genesis 17:5** when God says, "No longer shall your name be called Abram (exalted father), but your name shall be Abraham (father of a multitude); for I have made you the father of a multitude of nations."

Grammar and Syntax. These deal with the placement of words in sentences. In English, we place the adjective before the noun, as in "the red car." Spanish does the opposite, as in "el carro rojo" (the car red). This becomes important when trying to determine the emphasis of a passage. Which is more important, the "red" or the "car"? When we understand the normal structure of a language, we can more easily recognize when that structure has been changed for a specific reason. Grammar and syntax also tell us something about the writer's degree of education; his urban or rural upbringing; his exposure to outside influences, etc.

Gender. Is it male, female, or neutral? This has been hotly debated in light of recent gender-neutral translations that describe themselves as being "gender accurate." The idea behind such a translation is to use inclusive language to avoid the risk of anyone feeling excluded ("children" instead of "sons", etc.). In many cases, this is not such a big deal, however, in some cases this is a very big deal and can open the door for further doctrinal error. Consider what could happen to **John 3:16**: "For God so loved the world that He gave His only begotten Son…" compared to, "For God so loved the world that ("It") gave ("It's") only begotten ("Child")." Here is where solid, expository teaching is a must. We leave the gender as it is written and explain where the message includes everyone.

Formality. How formally do we address someone, especially God? Most of us are taught that there is a difference in how we address people in different stations of life. Titles of respect such as "Mr." or "Mrs.", "Sir" or "Ma'am" are often used to distinguish between our acquaintances, our elders, and our friends. When addressing God, the degree of formality has some real-life application. On the one hand, God is Holy and commands our utmost respect. On the other hand, He is our loving Father and wants our closest affection. Once again, context is crucial. It will often determine the degree of formality appropriate for the situation.

Before leaving translation, here are a few miscellaneous Bible features and facts that may be of interest:

Chapter and Verse Divisions. The chapter and verse divisions in both the Old and New Testaments are not part of the original Scripture, nor are the subject headings or titles that are found in many of our Bibles today. The verse divisions of the Old Testament were made by the Masoretes about 900 AD. Chapter divisions for the Old and New Testaments were made between 1244 and 1248 by Cardinal Hugo de Sancto Caro. Verse divisions for the New Testament were introduced by Robert Estienne in 1551. The first complete English Bible to contain our present chapter and verse divisions for both the Old and New Testaments was the Geneva Bible of 1560.

Study and Cross-Reference Bibles. These contain supplemental notes and cross-references to similar verses. The 1560 Geneva Bible is often credited as being the first English Bible that qualifies as a true study Bible. Although the notes and commentaries in a study Bible can be helpful at times, they are definitely not Scripture. The Bible is its own best commentary and a good cross-reference Bible can be very useful for comparing Scripture with other Scripture.

We should allow the Bible to speak for itself whenever and wherever possible.

Words of Christ in Red. The "red letter" is an innovation started by Louis Klopsch (1852-1910). On June 19, 1899, while composing an editorial, Mr. Klopsch came across **Luke 22:20**: "And in the same way He took the cup after they had eaten, saying, 'This cup which is poured out for you is the new covenant in My blood.'" Symbolizing the blood, he printed words that were thought to be spoken directly by Jesus in red. The red letter edition has been popular ever since.

Translations and Versions. The terms are used interchangeably but certain rules apply. By "translation," we mean going from the original language into other languages. Perhaps the most significant translation of the Old Testament is a Greek translation of the Hebrew, called the "Septuagint." This translation was produced in Egypt between 285-246 BC and was the one used by the early Christians. Many of the Old Testament quotations found in the New Testament are based on the Septuagint.

In order for a version to be considered a true translation it must be careful in certain areas. First, the Hebrew, Aramaic and Greek of the original text must be turned into modern speech while following normal rules of grammar. Second, a literal word-for-word approach should be used wherever possible. Technical words (such as 'propitiation', 'atonement', 'justification', etc.) must be kept intact. Third, cultural references should be maintained wherever possible. If these criteria are not met, the version is considered a paraphrase rather than a true translation.

We are often asked which Bible we personally recommend. For studying the Bible, and particularly for leading a group, we recommend using a literal translation. We believe that every word in the Bible was put there for a reason, whether for generations past, present, or future. Having said that, we must also acknowledge that the best Bible is the one that we will actually read. In light of this, we often recommend the following Bible for a balance of word-for-word accuracy and thought-for-thought readability: "**Today's Parallel Bible**" with NIV, KJV, NASB, NLT, published by Zondervan (ISBN 0-310-91836-7)).

Despite great opposition and debate, the Bible has stood the test of time. God's Word has remained an inspiration to countless millions and will continue to inspire millions to come. "The grass withers, the flower fades, but the word of our God stands forever." **(Isaiah 40:8)**

CHAPTER 3

BIBLE BASICS, PART 3

In this chapter, we outline the most common types of writing in the Old Testament. These include narrative, law, psalms, wisdom writings, and prophecy. Each type is unique, and each requires a different approach to fully understand the message being delivered.

NARRATIVE. Over 40% of the Old Testament is narrative, making it the most common type of literature in the entire Bible. A narrative is a story that purposefully re-tells the historical events of the past to give us meaning and direction in the present. When we say "story", we are not talking about a work of fiction like a children's book or a novel. Bible stories are actual, historical events that have been recorded as examples for us to learn from the past. "For whatever was written in earlier times was written for our instruction, so that through perseverance and the encouragement of the Scriptures we might have hope." **(Romans 15:4)**

All narratives have at least one character and at least one plot. Some of the elements to keep in mind are:

> **The Narrator.** Although usually not directly mentioned in the story, the narrator is everywhere and knows everything about the story he tells. Our only information comes from him. He decides what goes into the story and what does not. The narrator may choose not to share all that he knows and this can leave us wanting more information. The narrator is responsible for the point of view. The story is told from his perspective. In Hebrew story telling, the narrator does not typically explain, critique, or evaluate while telling the story. One of his main objectives is simply to tell the story in a way that allows us to see things for ourselves.

> **Scenes.** Bible scenes are often like those in a stage play. Hebrew narratives were more focused on scenes than on characters. Each scene stands alone, but their combination is what really makes the story come alive.

> **Characters**. These are often in contrast to each other. The use of opposites in characters is an

effective way to illustrate good and bad, wise and foolish, etc. Consider Cain and Abel **(Genesis 4)**, or Jacob and Esau **(Genesis 25)**. Remember that God Himself is the ultimate character and we should be on the lookout for His presence in the narrative. This is especially true when we see phrases like "but God." It has been said that "but God" indicates His divine intervention and is the hinge on which the door of history swings.

Dialogue. This is what the characters say. The dialogue gives insight into the characters' thoughts and motives. However, it is well understood that the spoken word comprises only 7% of all communication. Body language makes up 55%, tone of voice accounts for the remaining 38%. Sadly, much is lost when the dialogue is written on a page rather than acted out in front of our eyes.

Plot. Also known as the storyline, this is what the characters do. Hebrew narratives are typically fast paced, so we need to be on the lookout for devices that slow them down. Dialogue, commentary, historical background, etc. may all serve as the cues that direct us back to the main point of the story.

Structure. We must remember that for the most part, Scripture was passed along as spoken words to a listening audience. In general, the Bible was intended primarily for hearers, not for readers. As a result, repetition is a key ingredient. Repetition is a key ingredient. Repetition is a key ingredient.

When studying the Old Testament, there are some classic interpretation errors that should be avoided. Those most commonly made with narratives are:

Decontextualizing. This is taking a story out of its historical and literary context. An example would be for us to reference Ezra's rebuilding of the Temple in Jerusalem **(Ezra 1-10)** as God's affirmation for us to begin a new church building project.

Selecting. This is also known as picking and choosing. If we are honest, we must admit that there are parts of the Bible that we would rather leave out. Selecting is when we keep only the parts that we like while avoiding, ignoring, or removing the parts that we do not like.

Redefining. This is changing or stretching the meaning of a word or passage to suit our own agenda. Slightly different than selecting, redefining is trying to make the text say something that we want it to say rather than taking the text at its plain meaning.

Justifying. This is making reference to a bad or questionable example in an attempt to support bad or questionable behavior. Most of the characters in the Bible are far from perfect. We are not always told whether what happened was good or bad. Not all things in narratives are good examples for us. Just because we read that David had several wives or that Noah got drunk does not mean that God approved.

Allegorizing. This is looking too much for meanings beyond the text. We start seeing things as symbolic when they are not. A classic example is found in the writings of Augustine (354-430 AD). He interpreted the parable of the Good Samaritan **(Luke 10:25-37)** as follows: Jesus=the Good Samaritan, the donkey=the incarnate flesh, the inn=the Church, the innkeeper=Paul, etc. As we have said earlier, we believe that every word of the Bible is there for a reason. However, that reason may simply be to convey the message in a way that makes grammatical sense. No doubt, the Bible is filled with allegory. We just need to recognize when it is or when it is not being used. Not every word in Scripture has a hidden, underlying meaning.

LAW. Old Testament law is referred to as the Old Covenant or simply as "the Law." A covenant is a binding contract between two parties, spelling out the rights and responsibilities of each. It also describes any penalties associated with either party breaking the contract. There are two basic types of Old Testament laws:

1. **No-Contest.** These are laws that cannot be argued against because they have been proven to be logically true. No-contest laws are found in almost every culture across the globe. They deal with the things that every human being understands to be spiritually, morally, and socially wrong (murder, rape, stealing, etc.). The fact that we have no-contest law is a testimony to the fact that all mankind innately understands the difference between good and evil, right and wrong. It is also a testimony to the fact that we, collectively and individually, have a sin problem. We are lawbreakers at heart, in desperate need of forgiveness.

No-contest law has three main categories: Direct Commands, General Law, and Standards by Example.

Direct Commands typically begin with "do" or "do not" and include the famous "thou shalt not's" of the Ten Commandments. Although our tendency is to dwell on the negative (don't do this, don't do that), we really need to remember the positive. As believers, it's not enough for us not to do evil. Anyone can just sit and do nothing. Instead, we are called to be about our Father's business. We are called to do good.

General Law applies to the whole assembly of Israel. It describes what must always be done by every Israeli citizen in all situations. The observance of the mandatory feasts (Passover, Booths, etc.) is an example of General Law.

Standards by Example are illustrations of basic principles. When looking for loopholes, some will justify their position by saying that their particular situation was never specifically addressed in the Bible. Again, we believe that the Bible contains all of the necessary direction we need for every situation we may face in this life. Where there is no direct statement made for a particular situation, Standards by Example give us definite principles and guidelines that can be applied to it. Paul illustrates this concept when he writes, "Who at any time serves as a soldier at his own expense? Who plants a vineyard and does not eat the fruit of it? Or who tends a flock and does not use the milk of the flock? I am not speaking these things according to human judgment, am I? Or does not the Law also say these things? For it is written in the Law of Moses, 'You shall not muzzle the ox while he is threshing.' God is not concerned about oxen, is He? Or is He speaking altogether for our sake? Yes, for our sake it was written, because the plowman ought to plow in hope, and the thresher ought to thresh in hope of sharing the crops." **(1 Corinthians 9:7-10)**

2. **Case-by-Case**. These laws single out particular cases that apply only to some people in some situations. An example of case-by-case law is found in **Numbers 27:2-11** when the daughters of Zelophehad "stood before Moses and before Eleazar the priest and before

the leaders and all the congregation, at the doorway of the tent of meeting, saying, 'Our father died in the wilderness, yet he was not among the company of those who gathered themselves together against the LORD in the company of Korah; but he died in his own sin, and he had no sons. Why should the name of our father be withdrawn from among his family because he had no son? Give us a possession among our father's brothers.' So Moses brought their case before the LORD. Then the LORD spoke to Moses, saying, 'The daughters of Zelophehad are right in their statements. You shall surely give them a hereditary possession among their father's brothers, and you shall transfer the inheritance of their father to them. Further, you shall speak to the sons of Israel, saying, 'If a man dies and has no son, then you shall transfer his inheritance to his daughter. If he has no daughter, then you shall give his inheritance to his brothers. If he has no brothers, then you shall give his inheritance to his father's brothers. If his father has no brothers, then you shall give his inheritance to his nearest relative in his own family, and he shall possess it; and it shall be a statutory ordinance to the sons of Israel, just as the LORD commanded Moses.'"

So, the real question is how does Old Testament law apply to us today? In short, the Old Covenant served as a tutor to point us to Jesus. He has fulfilled the requirements of the Law on our behalf. Here, it is best simply to let Scripture speak for itself.

Jesus said, "Do not think that I came to abolish the Law or the Prophets; I did not come to abolish but to fulfill. For truly I say to you, until heaven and earth pass away, not the smallest letter or stroke shall pass from the Law until all is accomplished. Whoever then annuls one of the least of these commandments, and teaches others to do the same, shall be called least in the kingdom of heaven; but whoever keeps and teaches them, he shall be called great in the kingdom of heaven." **(Matthew 5:17-19)**

"But now we have been released from the Law, having died to that by which we were bound, so that we serve in newness of the Spirit and not in oldness of the letter." **(Romans 7:6)**

"Is the Law then contrary to the promises of God? May it never be! For if a Law had been given which was able to impart life, then righteousness would indeed have been based on law. But the Scripture has shut up everyone under sin, so that the promise by faith in Jesus Christ might be given to those who believe. But before faith came, we were kept in custody under the law, being shut up to the faith which was later to be revealed. Therefore the Law has become our tutor to lead us to Christ, so that we may be justified by faith. But now that faith has come, we are no longer under a tutor. For you are all sons of God through faith in Christ Jesus." **(Galatians 3:21-26)**

The Old Testament is not our testament. The gospels make it clear that "…in the same way (Jesus) took the cup after they had eaten, saying, 'This cup which is poured out for you is the new covenant in My blood.'" **(Luke 22:20)** As a result, we are not bound to any of the Old Testament laws unless they are actually repeated again in the New Testament. That is simply the nature of covenant law. Similar to a rental agreement, once the new contract is established, the old contract is discarded and we are no longer bound to any of it. The new contract may contain many of the same items as the old one, but it is still a completely different document and must be treated as such.

Although the Old Testament law is not God's direct command *to* us now, it is still God's word *for* us now. He still expects our devotion and obedience. It is the expression of that devotion and obedience that has been changed.

Some Old Testament laws that are not renewed in the New Testament include:

> **Civil Laws**. Also known as the "law of the land." These specify the penalties for various crimes for which one might be arrested and tried in Israel. Civil law is concerned with a citizen's relationship to a specific culture and government. If we travel to another country, we are expected to obey the law of that land regardless of our own nationality. Depending on the country, there may be different laws that apply to citizens versus non-citizens.

> **Ritual Laws.** These are rules for worship and sacrifice. Although rituals make up the largest part of un-renewed Old Testament law, they are also the most actively misapplied today. The misapplication can often be traced to the assumption that the New Testament is somehow less demanding or pious than the Old Testament. In reality, the opposite is true. Take "tithing" for example. Tithing (the giving of 10%) is not renewed in the New Testament. We are absolutely not obligated to tithe. However, under the New Testament, we are

obligated to "give." At first, this seems pretty easy. That is until we realize that giving is actually much more demanding than tithing. God expects us to be good stewards of 100%, not just 10%. Genuine New Testament giving is a 24-hour-a-day, 7-day-a-week personal commitment to a lifestyle of honoring God with all of our resources. Rituals can become dead, mechanical, and meaningless. Genuine faith, however, comes from the heart and finds its way into the very fabric of our being such that we cannot help but live it out through every aspect of our lives.

Some Old Testament laws that are renewed in the New Testament include:

The 10 Commandments (Exodus 20:1-17). These are repeated in various ways in the New Testament **(Matthew 5:21-37, Mark 10:17-19**, etc.). The specifics about keeping the Sabbath, however, have been changed **(Matthew 12, etc.)**.

Ethical Laws. These support the two basic laws of the New Covenant. "On these two commandments depend the whole Law and the Prophets" (**Matthew 22:40**). In short, ethical law includes:

Loving God. "You shall love the Lord your God with all your heart, and with all your soul, and with all your mind." **(Matthew 22:37, Deuteronomy**

6:5). This is our vertical relationship between man and God.

Loving People. "You shall love your neighbor as yourself." **(Matthew 22:39, Leviticus 19:18).** This is our horizontal relationship between man and fellow man.

Laws of Character. These are qualities that are always good, all the time. Godly character displays the fruit of the Spirit, which is "love, joy, peace, patience, kindness, goodness, faithfulness, gentleness, self-control; against such things there is no law." **(Galatians 5:22-23)**

PSALMS. Described as musical poems, *"psalms"* (or *"psalters"*) originally referred to a specific type of stringed instrument, then later to the songs that were played on that instrument. Psalms are intended to appeal to the emotions. They engage the mind through the heart. Psalms are written to express our feelings to God or about God. Every facet of human emotion (our joy, sorrow, success, failure, etc.) can be found within the Psalms. In a beautiful and artistic way, the psalms show us that we can be completely honest with God about our deepest thoughts and feelings.

Each psalm contains its own complete message and is intended to stand on its own. Even so, a psalm may refer to other psalms. Just like our music today, different psalms have different rhythms, tempos, lyrics, themes, etc. Sadly, we are only given the words to the psalms without the accompanying music. We are sometimes given notes for the musical director at the beginning of a psalm, but we still don't get the full picture. Much is lost, especially considering how the music alone can make us feel joy or sorrow simply by the key in which it is played. In addition, rhyme schemes and word plays can get lost in translation (if you have ever heard your favorite song in another language, then you understand – it just doesn't sound quite right).

Below are some terms that we come across when reading the Psalms. The definite meanings of most of these terms have been lost to history. We are almost positive that they are some kind of instruction as to how the song should be played, but much of the language lends itself to several possible interpretations.

> **Maskil.** May mean "instructional," "contemplative," or "skillful."
> **Mikhtam**. May indicate a private memorial or a short psalm that ends with an unexpected twist of thought.
> **Selah**. *"Lifting up."* May mean the raising of the voice or a dramatic pause.

An "acrostic" is a special type of poetry in which the first letter of each line spells out a word or a message. There are several acrostics throughout the Bible, most notably, **Psalm 119** whose subsections correspond to each letter of the Hebrew alphabet.

WISDOM WRITINGS. "Wisdom" is truth and good judgment put into action. It is the ability to make Godly choices in life.

"The fear of the Lord is the beginning of wisdom, and the knowledge of the Holy One is understanding." **(Proverbs 9:10)** Wisdom is the practical application of knowledge, not just the knowledge itself. Most of us agree that it is better to be wise than smart. Intellectual knowledge is only helpful when we can rightly apply it to our lives. Ultimately, the goal of true, Biblical knowledge is for us to become more like Christ. Peter explains it this way: "Grace and peace be multiplied to you in the knowledge of God and of Jesus our Lord; seeing that His divine power has granted to us everything pertaining to life and godliness, through the true knowledge of Him who called us by His own glory and excellence. For by these He has granted to us His precious and magnificent promises, so that by them you may become partakers of the divine nature, having escaped the corruption that is in the world by lust. Now for this very reason also, applying all diligence, in your faith supply moral excellence, and in your moral excellence, knowledge, and in your knowledge, self-control, and in your self-control, perseverance, and in your perseverance, godliness, and in your godliness, brotherly kindness, and in your brotherly kindness, love. For if these qualities are yours and are increasing, they render you neither useless nor unfruitful in the true knowledge of our Lord Jesus Christ." **(2 Peter 1:2-8)**

We tend to think that to be wise is to know everything. In fact, the opposite is true. The Bible almost always equates wisdom with the ability to receive and to apply instruction. As a result, we are always in the process of learning. Only "fools despise wisdom and instruction." **(Proverbs 1:7)** But, "give instruction to a wise man and he will be still wiser, Teach a righteous man and he will increase his learning." **(Proverbs 9:9)** "A poor yet wise lad is better than an old and foolish king who no longer knows how to receive instruction." **(Ecclesiastes 4:13)** We must always be willing not only to receive God's instruction, but to allow ourselves to be changed by it as well.

Wisdom writings are full of proverbs and figures of speech. These are short, popular sayings that express a common truth or a useful thought. A proverb is easier to remember than a technical explanation. For example, "Look before you leap" versus, "Before engaging in any action that may cause harm, we should take time to analyze the potential risks and outcomes of such an action before we commit to its undertaking." Proverbial sayings and idioms (where the actual meaning goes beyond the words themselves) are so integrated into our language and culture that idioms are often used to explain other idioms.

PROPHECY. When we hear the word "prophecy," we almost immediately think "future." However, the primary function of the prophet was to speak for God to his own people, in his own time, confronting them with God's law, with sin, and with the need for repentance. In a manner of speaking, the prophet had a similar ministry as that of the Holy Spirit to "convict the world concerning sin and righteousness and judgment." **(John 16:8)** The prophets served as watchmen for the people as described in **Ezekiel 33**, and "it was revealed to (them) that they were not serving themselves, but you, in these things which now have been announced to you through those who preached the gospel to you by the Holy Spirit sent from heaven - things into which angels long to look." **(1 Peter 1:12)**

The secondary role of the prophet was to foretell events before they happened. Foretelling is very different from predicting. There is no guessing involved in foretelling. When a prophet spoke, it came to pass. This assurance was a sign that the prophet was truly from God. The foretelling of the future gave credibility to the prophets' message of repentance.

The Old Testament prophetic books were all written between 760 and 460 BC. They are most often distinguished by the size of the books ("Major" or "Minor"). The Major Prophets include Isaiah, Jeremiah, Ezekiel, and Daniel. The Minor Prophets include the final 12 books of the Old Testament. Ancient Judaism combined these into one book, referred to as "The Book of the Twelve", or simply as, "The Twelve". Although we tend to classify according to size, it often helps to look at Old Testament prophecy in terms of its relation to the Exile. The "Exile", or Babylonian captivity, ran in stages from 608 to 538 BC. With the exception of the Exodus, the Exile was perhaps the most defining, pivotal event in Israel's Old Testament history. We have a different perspective when we know that judgment is coming, versus when we are living in the middle of it, versus when we are looking back at it.

When studying any prophetic writing, the background of the book is extremely important. Dates, people, places, nations, culture, religion, politics, etc., all play an important role in understanding the prophecies and the prophets themselves. Why did God use this prophet, at this time, to deliver this message, to this group of people? Although we often try to write ourselves into it, Old Testament prophecy usually dealt with the immediate or near future of Israel, Judah, and other surrounding nations. Ultimately, all prophecy (Old and New

Testament) revolves around the Messiah and God's redemptive work in His people.

John the Baptist was the last of the Old Testament prophets. Jesus testified about him by declaring, "What did you go out into the wilderness to see? A reed shaken by the wind? But what did you go out to see? A man dressed in soft clothing? Those who wear soft clothing are in kings' palaces! But what did you go out to see? A prophet? Yes, I tell you, and one who is more than a prophet. This is the one about whom it is written, 'Behold, I send My messenger ahead of You, who will prepare Your way before You.' Truly I say to you, among those born of women there has not arisen anyone greater than John the Baptist! Yet the one who is least in the kingdom of heaven is greater than he. From the days of John the Baptist until now the kingdom of heaven suffers violence, and violent men take it by force. For all the prophets and the Law prophesied until John. And if you are willing to accept it, John himself is Elijah who was to come. He who has ears to hear, let him hear.'" **(Matthew 11:7-15)**

John the Baptist was the greatest because he was the only prophet who could directly, physically point to Jesus, the Messiah, and say, "Behold, the Lamb of God who takes away the sin of the world!" **(John 1:29)** Before John, the Old Testament prophets could only say, "I see him, but not now; I behold him, but not near; a star shall come forth from Jacob, a scepter shall rise from Israel…" **(Numbers 24:17)**

CHAPTER 4

BIBLE BASICS, PART 4

In this chapter, we outline the most common types of writing in the New Testament. These include gospels, parables, narratives, epistles, and apocalypse. Each type is unique, and each requires a different approach to fully understand the message being delivered.

GOSPELS. "For I am not ashamed of the gospel, for it is the power of God for salvation to everyone who believes…" **(Romans 1:16)**

    "Gospel" (euaggélion - evangelism) simply means "good news." When we say, "the" Gospel, what we are actually saying is "the" Good News. In other words, whatever good news we may have heard before, this news, "the" Gospel, tops it all.

So what exactly is this good news? Simply put, "…that Christ died for our sins according to the Scriptures, and that He was buried, and that He was raised on the third day according to the Scriptures…" **(1 Corinthians 15:3-4)** In other words, the gospel is the forgiveness of our sin through the death and resurrection of Jesus.

We must be careful not to shorten the Gospel to the fact that Jesus died for our sin. That is a nice thought, but there is no power in it (people die every day). The power of the Gospel is in the fact that Jesus rose again. There is an empty tomb in Jerusalem. And because He lives, we know that we who have believed in Him will also live. For "all of us who have been baptized into Christ Jesus have been baptized into His death. Therefore we have been buried with Him through baptism into death, so that as Christ was raised from the dead through the glory of the Father, so we too might walk in newness of life. For if we have become united with Him in the likeness of His death, certainly we shall also be in the likeness of His resurrection, knowing this, that our old self was crucified with Him, in order that our body of sin might be done away with, so that we would no longer be slaves to sin; for he who has died is freed from sin. Now if we have died with Christ, we believe that we shall also live with Him…" **(Romans 6:3-8)**

The Gospel revolves around the person of Jesus - what He said, and what He did. There have been many articulate men throughout the ages, but none as perfectly eloquent or as true as Jesus. When we consider that He is the Word that "became flesh and dwelt among us" **(John 1:14)**, it is no wonder that He always had the right thing to say at the right time. But Jesus is more than just a philosopher or a man with some clever sayings. He is the very Word of God in the flesh. When He spoke, "the crowds were amazed at His teaching; for He was teaching them as one having authority, and not as their scribes." **(Matthew 7:29)** Of His teaching, Jesus Himself said, "If anyone hears My sayings and does not keep them, I do not judge him; for I did not come to judge the world, but to save the world. He who rejects Me and does not receive My sayings, has one who judges him; the word I spoke is what will judge him at the last day. For I did not speak on My own initiative, but the Father Himself who sent Me has given Me a commandment as to what to say and what to speak. I know that His commandment is eternal life; therefore the things I speak, I speak just as the Father has told Me." **(John 12:47-50)** As countless millions can testify, "never has a man spoken the way this man speaks." **(John 7:46)**

The biography of Jesus is a limited one. Some events are recorded in great detail, while others are nearly silent. As John puts it, "there are also many other things which Jesus did, which if they were written in detail, I suppose that even the world itself would not contain the books that would be written." **(John 21:25)** Once again, it helps to understand the purpose of the writing. Why were some things included while others were not? Luke wrote his gospel "so that you may know the exact truth about the things you have been taught." **(Luke 1:4)** John, on the other hand, wrote "so that you may believe that Jesus is the Christ, the Son of God; and that believing you may have life in His name." **(John 20:31)**

So why do we have four gospels? In short, they allow us to see four different sides of the same story. As a result, we have a more complete picture of the singular Gospel of Jesus

Christ. We all respond differently to various styles of presentation. Some of us are more artistic, some more scientific, some more philosophical, etc. Considering the importance of the message, it is no surprise that each gospel has its own unique style, allowing each of us the opportunity to hear the same message in a way that makes sense to our own unique personality. As Paul would say, "To the Jews I became as a Jew, so that I might win Jews; to those who are under the Law, as under the Law though not being myself under the Law, so that I might win those who are under the Law; to those who are without law, as without law, though not being without the law of God but under the law of Christ, so that I might win those who are without law. To the weak I became weak, that I might win the weak; I have become all things to all men, so that I may by all means save some." **(1 Corinthians 9:20-22)**

The Gospel according to Matthew serves as a bridge between the Old and New Testaments. With a Jewish audience in mind, Matthew focuses on Jesus as the Messiah, the fulfillment of Old Testament prophecy.

Mark is short and to the point. The Gospel according to Mark is thought to be the first gospel written. Geared toward a Gentile (non-Jewish) audience, it places emphasis on miracles and on Jesus as a powerful, obedient Man of action.

Luke's gospel is an orderly prequel to the book of Acts. Also geared toward a Gentile audience, Luke gives us the life and ministry of Jesus in a systematic and straightforward way.

Of the four gospels, John is the most evangelical. Written to compel people to come to faith in Christ, the gospel of John focuses on theology and on Jesus as being both "Son of God" and "Son of Man."

The gospels are not in chronological order. They were not written to give us a step-by-step account of the life and teachings of Jesus. Although Luke attempted to write things in consecutive order, even he did not hold to a perfectly chronological record. For perspective, we could compare the gospels to conversations at the funeral of a close friend. Each of us could recall memories of our time spent together, but some of us would remember childhood events, while others would tell of more recent times. Each of those memories would trigger additional memories, but not in any particular order. Three of the gospels (Matthew, Mark, and Luke) are referred to as "synoptic" (meaning, "seeing together") because they frequently overlap each other. By comparing these overlaps, we get a more complete picture of how and when the events took place.

PARABLES. "All these things Jesus spoke to the crowds in parables, and He did not speak to them without a parable. This was to fulfill what was spoken through the prophet: 'I will open My mouth in parables; I will utter things hidden since the foundation of the world.'" **(Matthew 13:34-35)**

A parable (literally, "setting alongside of") is an earthly story with a heavenly meaning. However, not all 'parables' are parables. A true parable is one that has a beginning, a plot, and an ending. A classic example is that of the prodigal son in **Luke 15:11-32**. If it does not have a beginning, plot, and ending, then we are dealing with a metaphor, simile, or other comparison. These figures of speech are very closely related to proverbs and include the famous "the kingdom of heaven is like…" parables of **Matthew 13**.

A parable never perfectly represents the real thing. For example, a friend just remembered some obscure fact and proudly declares that he is "like an elephant" (an animal known for its excellent memory). We could carry that comparison on to many areas: floppy ears, long nose, big teeth, wrinkled skin, weighing several tons, etc. Obviously, this is not what our friend had in mind when making the comparison. We must be careful not to read too far into the symbolism.

A parable's function is to bring out a natural response or reaction from the hearer. In some ways, interpreting a parable kills its impact much like interpreting a joke to someone who doesn't get it. The impact of a parable depends on its points of reference. These are the parts of the story with which we can identify because they are part of our culture or common experience. A funny story involving a horse and a diving board is not very funny to someone who is not familiar with a horse or a diving board. An effective parable brings the points of reference to an unanticipated conclusion. But this unexpected twist only works if the hearer understands the points of reference. Otherwise, it's like a punch line separated from the joke.

Parables are audience dependent. How a parable is received depends on the perspective of the hearer. The same parable can mean different things to different people. This is what we refer to as the "double-edged sword" of Scripture. An excellent example is found in **Luke 7:36-50**. In this parable, there are at least three distinct hearers: a Pharisee named Simon, an immoral woman, and those who were at the table with them. By the end, each one came away with a different but altogether correct interpretation. To Simon, conviction; to the woman, forgiveness; and to the others, the revelation that Jesus has the authority to forgive sins. One story, several truths, multiple reactions. This is the beauty of the parable.

We are often frustrated by parables. After all, if God wanted the message to be clear, why not give it to us in plain language? The disciples had the same frustration. "And (they) came and said to Him, 'Why do you speak to them in parables?' Jesus answered them, 'To you it has been granted to know the mysteries of the kingdom of heaven, but to them it has not been granted. For whoever has, to him more shall be given, and he will have an abundance; but whoever does not have, even what he has shall be taken away from him. Therefore I speak to them in parables; because while seeing they do not see, and while hearing they do not hear, nor do they understand. In their case the prophecy of Isaiah is being fulfilled, which says, "You will keep on hearing, but will not understand; you will keep on seeing, but will not perceive; for the heart of this people has become dull, with their ears they scarcely hear, and they have closed their eyes, otherwise they would see with their eyes, hear with their ears, and understand with their heart and return, and I would heal them." But blessed are your eyes, because they see; and your ears, because they hear. For truly I say to you that many prophets and righteous men desired to see what you see, and did not see it, and to hear what you hear, and did not hear it.'" **(Matthew 13:10-17)** The main purpose of a parable is to reveal truth to those who seek it while hiding it from those who don't. "He who has ears to hear, let him hear." **(Mark 4:9, Luke 14:35, etc.)**

NARRATIVE. Mostly concentrated in the book of Acts, New Testament narrative tells historical events of the past to give us meaning and direction in the present. Among other things, New Testament narrative gives us the context and framework for many of the New Testament letters (epistles). Whenever we study a letter, we should turn to the appropriate narrative for its context. For example, if we are studying Philippians, a look at **Acts 16** will show us how the Church at Philippi began. This type of cross-referencing will answer many of our who, what, when, where, and why questions.

New Testament narrative also gives us a picture of what the early Church was like and how the early believers lived out their faith. It is extremely important to understand that many of the things that were written were specific to that particular group of people at that particular point in time. Although these narratives contain many principles and ideas that may be applied today, we must acknowledge the fact that God continues to work with and through His people in ways that are relevant to the times, cultures, and places in which His Church resides. We must be careful not to confuse "religious culture" (those norms and customs that are typical of various eras and congregations throughout the history of the Church) with sound Christian doctrine. As a general rule, sound doctrine can be viewed as that which was taught by Jesus, was practiced in the book of Acts, and was expounded on in the epistles. If all three parameters are not met, then we are most likely dealing with a non-essential tradition rather than with a fundamental Christian doctrine.

EPISTLES. An "epistle" simply means a letter. Typically, we refer to a letter as an epistle only when it was written as an instruction or exhortation to the Church. Since they were usually addressed to a general audience, epistles were more formal than personal letters. Most of them were shared and read aloud among the various congregations, as we see in **Colossians 4:16** ("When this letter is read among you, have it also read in the church of the Laodiceans; and you, for your part read my letter that is coming from Laodicea").

As with narratives, the subject matter within the epistles may be general (for all believers, for all time) or specific (for those believers, for that time). Some of the passages were written to address specific issues that are permanently linked to the specific context of the writing. We must take great care in how we apply such passages to our own lives, lest we fall into the same trap as that of the Pharisees and find ourselves "transgressing the commandment of God for the sake of (our) traditions" and "teaching as doctrines the precepts of men." **(Matthew 15:3,9)**

In His infinite wisdom and creative genius, God preserves the personalities of His people. We are not robots. Nor were the writers of the New Testament. The Bible was written by "men moved by the Holy Spirit spoke from God." **(2 Peter 1:21)** Though rightfully held in high regard, these men were just men. As such, each writer brings his own style and personality to the letter. And, every once in a while, some opinions do come into play. For example, Paul stated such things as, "…I have no command of the Lord, but I give an opinion…" **(1 Corinthians 7:25)** or, "but to the rest I say, not the Lord..." **(1 Corinthians 7:12)** The fact that God preserves the character of His people even in the writing of His Word is not a negative. Rather, it serves as a powerful testimony to His intimate knowledge of humanity and to His love for each of us as individuals.

APOCALYPSE. True apocalypse is an extinct form of Jewish and Christian writing that appeared from about 200 BC to 350 AD. The word, "apocalypse" (apokálupsis), or "revelation" simply means, "to reveal or to uncover." Apocalyptic writing deals with the end times in which the forces of good permanently triumph over the forces of evil.

The Book of Revelation is the most familiar of the New Testament apocalyptic writings. Given to the apostle John around 95 AD while exiled on the island of Patmos, the Revelation is a unique combination of apocalypse, prophecy, and epistle. It is important to note that the writing is "the (singular) Revelation of Jesus Christ," and not "Revelations" (plural). This might seem like a minor point, but it has a lot to do with the main focus of the book being not on multiple future events, but rather on the singular person of Jesus Christ. "The (singular) testimony of Jesus is the (singular) spirit of prophecy." **(Revelation 19:10)** Though in some ways difficult to understand, the book begins with the promise that "blessed is he who reads and those who hear the words of the prophecy, and heed the things which are written in it; for the time is near." **(Revelation 1:3)**. The book ends, however, with a solemn warning "to everyone who hears the words of the prophecy of this book: if anyone adds to them, God will add to him the plagues which are written in this book; and if anyone takes away from the words of the book of this prophecy, God will take away his part from the tree of life and from the holy city, which are written in this book." **(Revelation 22:18-19)**

New Testament apocalypse often directly refers to, or uses similar language as that of the Old Testament. This is why we go back to those original Old Testament prophecies to see how it all ties together. For quick reference, many of today's Bibles print Old Testament quotes in all capital letters or in a different font than their surrounding New Testament passages.

We must remember that the apocalyptic authors wrote from their own place and time. To illustrate the future, they could refer only to what was available to them from their past and present, not from ours. When trying to figure out to whom or to what the writer may be referring, we have to understand that objects of modern times were unavailable to the apocalyptic writers. They would not have known about automobiles, air travel, computers, cell phones, or nuclear weapons. If in a vision they saw such things, they would not have had specific words for them. They would only have had their best descriptions. In addition, they would not have known (except in cases of extremely detailed revelation) the names of countries or of political leaders that did not yet exist.

In our desire to understand and prepare for the future, many can become bogged down and preoccupied with the details of eschatology (the study of the end times). Even though Jesus Himself told us that no one would know the day nor the hour of His return **(Matthew 24:36; Mark 13:32)**, the time-line of the second coming of Christ remains one of the most studied and heated topics in all of Christendom. Regardless of our position, it all boils down to two fundamental, undeniable truths: **1)** Jesus is coming; and **2)** Be ready. Consider this the end times made simple.

CHAPTER 5

BIBLE BASICS, PART 5

In a world marked by constant change, mankind has, throughout history, sought after those things that are unchanging. We have sought after truth, not only as that for which we are willing to die, but as that for which we are willing to live. Man's internal battle with absolutes was the same in Jesus' day, and we catch a glimpse of it in **John 18:37-38** when "Pilate said to Him, 'So You are a king?' Jesus answered, 'You say correctly that I am a king. For this I have been born, and for this I have come into the world, to testify to the truth. Everyone who is of the truth hears My voice.' Pilate said to Him, 'What is truth?'"

Pilate's question, "What is truth?" is perhaps the most depressing and hopeless question that anyone could ever ask, yet it remains one of the most frequently asked questions even today. Heaven's response is timeless and straightforward: "If you continue in My word, then you are truly disciples of Mine; and you will know the truth, and the truth will make you free." **(John 8:31-32)**

This chapter outlines the basic principles for studying the Bible with consistency and accuracy. Rather than memorizing random facts or analyzing specific doctrines, our goal is to condition ourselves to "think" theologically. Once we establish an appropriate system of thought, we can approach any theological or doctrinal issue with a certain degree of confidence that we are "accurately handling the word of truth." **(2 Timothy 2:15)**

Every single one of us has a belief system that is entirely based upon our view of God. Although we try to avoid it, we are nevertheless forced to confront our theology on an almost daily basis. "Theology" simply means, "the study of God," and the branch of theology concerned with the defense or validity of Christianity is called "apologetics" (literally, "a formal defense"). Knowing what we believe and why we believe it is not nearly as difficult as most of us first assume. We are instructed simply to "...sanctify Christ as Lord in (our) hearts, always being ready to make a defense to everyone who asks (us) to give an account for the hope that is in (us), yet with gentleness and reverence..." **(1 Peter 3:15)**

Whether we know it or not, whether we like it or not, every single one of us has a belief system - a "theology" - be it Christianity, or atheism, or anything in between. Everyone has an opinion about God even if that opinion is favorable, antagonistic, or apathetic. Ultimately, our belief system is what drives each of us to do what we do. Our theology only becomes formalized when our beliefs are challenged or questioned by others or by ourselves. Over the years, formal Christian theology has branched into three main categories: Historical, Biblical, and Systematic.

Historical theology is the study of the progression of beliefs throughout the history of the Church. Historical theology is just that – historical. This type of approach looks at church movements, cultural shifts, reformations, etc. It considers the flow of doctrine as it passes from one Church generation to the next. As such, historical theology is affected by popular culture even within Christian circles. Things that may be acceptable in this generation may have been completely intolerable only two generations ago. Although useful for appreciating how far we have come in thought and understanding, historical theology can be prone to relativism (the false belief that if doctrine changes over time, we can never establish any permanent truth).

Biblical theology is the study of a particular writer or book of the Bible. It asks such questions as "What did Peter believe?" or "What does the book of James teach?" and it generally stays within the boundaries of the particular writer or book. Biblical theology is useful for understanding and appreciating different perspectives of different authors, but it can be prone to isolating scripture out of context. A close cousin to Biblical theology is denominational theology, the espousing of complete sets of doctrines from later Christian writers (Calvin, Arminius, Luther, Wesley, etc.). Many of our larger denominations have stemmed from this branch of theology. Even if someone does have tremendous insight into Scripture and doctrine, we must be careful not to elevate individuals who are but men. We follow Christ alone. If we are prone to label ourselves, then that label must always be that of a "Christian" first and foremost over any denominational affiliation we may hold. Paul addresses this very issue when he writes, "Now I exhort you, brethren, by the name of our Lord Jesus Christ, that you all agree and that there be no divisions among you, but that you be made complete in the same mind and in the same judgment. For I have been informed concerning you, my brethren, by Chloe's people, that there are quarrels among you. Now I mean this, that each one of you is saying, 'I am of Paul,' and 'I of Apollos,' and 'I of Cephas,' and 'I of Christ.' Has Christ been divided? Paul was not crucified for you, was he? Or were you baptized in the name of Paul?" **(1 Corinthians 1:10-13)**

That brings us to **Systematic** theology. Systematic theology is the attempt to take a comprehensive look at everything that the Bible says about a given subject in an effort to develop certain foundational truths about that subject. Systematic theology employs various rules of logic and research to assure that conclusions do not contradict themselves or each other. This approach utilizes information from every possible credible source including the Bible, archaeology, science, history, etc., and it follows in the spirit of the Bereans who "were more noble-minded than those in Thessalonica, for they received the word with great eagerness, examining the Scriptures daily to see whether these things were so." **(Acts 17:10-11)**

Faith and logic are the two fundamental principles of systematic theology. Contrary to popular belief, faith is not blind.

Rather, it is "the substance of things hoped for, the evidence of things not seen."**(Hebrews 11:1)** The honest study of God uses logic and elements of scientific method in a systematic, organized way that compliments our faith. God is the Creator of the human mind, and faith and logic do go hand in hand as is clearly seen in **John 1:1**, "In the beginning was the 'Word'" ('logos' ('thought'), from which we derive "logic"). Genuine faith does not require us to leave our brains behind, nor does genuine logic require us to contradict our calling to "walk by faith, not by sight." **(2 Corinthians 5:7)** In His infinite love and wisdom, God has given every man the measure of faith. **(Romans 12:3)** In fact, faith is displayed by every single person on a daily basis, even if that person doesn't believe in it. When was the last time we thought about breathing or gravity, or when did we last test load a chair before we sat down on it? Ultimately, faith is based on trust, and trust is based on consistency. We learn to trust those things that have been consistently proven to be trustworthy. This is one of the fundamental cornerstones of scientific method – the ability to demonstrate repeated, consistent outcomes. Certainly, God meets that criterion "For I, the Lord, do not change…" **(Malachi 3:6)**, and "Jesus Christ is the same yesterday and today and forever." **(Hebrews 13:8)**

However, we must also be careful not to limit God's infinite logic to our own finite understanding. "'For My thoughts are not your thoughts, Nor are your ways My ways,' declares the LORD. 'For as the heavens are higher than the earth, so are My ways higher than your ways and My thoughts than your thoughts.'" **(Isaiah 55:8-9)** There may be times when God directs us to trust Him in ways that we do not fully understand, or in ways which, at least on the surface, seem to contradict His Word (for example, **Acts 10**, where Peter is commanded to eat unclean food; or **Hosea 1** where God commands the prophet to marry a prostitute). The sovereignty of God surpasses human logic, "so that (our) faith would not rest on the wisdom of men, but on the power of God." **(1 Corinthians 2:5)**

The Bible is our standard and God's Word is always the final authority. When our personal beliefs contradict the Bible, we change our beliefs. "Let God be found true, though every man be found a liar…" **(Romans 3:4)** In Chapters 1 & 2, we spent a great deal of time establishing the credibility of the Bible. Scripture is like 'north' on the compass. It keeps us pointed in the right direction. We may not always like where north happens to be pointing, but north is north nonetheless. If we change it, we end up lost and confused, miles away from where we need to be. Simply put, truth is truth because it is true.

Though Biblical knowledge is essential for a healthy Christian walk, the ultimate goal of theology is application. In the end, we live out what we truly believe. **Mark 9:14-24** tells the story of a man with a demon-possessed son. This passage is an excellent example of practical atheism. If we are honest, most of us can relate to the man's statement, "I do believe; help my unbelief!" In other words, we believe up to a certain point before our faith gives way to doubt. We may say that our faith surpasses that point, but like it or not, our actions will always give us away. It is not until our faith is tested that we truly know its limits. As God continues to challenge our faith through His Word, our hope is to be men and women who allow ourselves to be molded and shaped "to become conformed to the image of His Son." **(Romans 8:29)**

A theology, or "belief system," contains many specific, individual doctrines. "Doctrine" simply means "teaching." Our beliefs about baptism, gifts of the Spirit, heaven and hell, church leadership, etc., are all specific doctrines within our broader theology. Some of these doctrines are absolutely essential, while others are not. Depending on our spiritual background, most of us embrace a personal mix of doctrines that do not fall neatly into one standardized theology. As a result, we have many different denominations within Christianity. One common creed among believers says, "In essentials, unity. In non-essentials, liberty. In all things, love." The difficulty, of course, is in determining which doctrines are essential to the Faith. In other words, what makes a Christian a Christian?

As we develop our theology, we face the issue of doctrinal harmony. In essence, we want to know how our doctrines fit together. For example, Jesus said, "God is spirit, and those who worship Him must worship in spirit *and* truth." **(John 4:24)** Notice that He did not say, "spirit *or* truth." Both elements must be present and functioning together. All too often, we hold onto one at the exclusion of the other. This is where doctrinal harmony comes into play. How can two seemingly opposite doctrines both be true? Think of such classic debates as predestination vs. free will, etc. Perhaps the best analogy is that of a cone. When viewed in two dimensions, a three dimensional cone can appear to be either a triangle or a circle depending on the perspective.

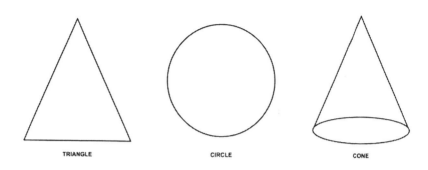

TRIANGLE   CIRCLE   CONE

Our individual circumstances might not allow us to comprehend both perspectives at the same time. God, however, has infinitely more dimensions and perspectives than we do. We live in time, He *created* time. We feel love, He *is* love. When faced with two equally viable options, we must always be prepared to look for a third. Viewing theology from all possible angles is not an easy task, but it is a necessary one, especially when attempting to explain the truth upon which we stake our very lives.

Doctrinal harmony consists of two parts: Internal and External. **Internal** harmony looks at consistency within a doctrine itself. Is there unity among the various Scriptures that teach on the same subject? Consider the doctrine of "substitutionary atonement" (the payment for our sin by the blood of something or someone other than ourselves). **Hebrews 9:22** tells us that "according to the Law, one may almost say, all things are cleansed with blood, and without shedding of blood there is no forgiveness." In the Old Testament, we see the blood of animals shed to pay for the sin of man. In the New Testament, we see the blood of a Savior shed on our behalf. We are redeemed "with precious blood, as of a lamb unblemished and spotless, the blood of Christ." **(1 Peter 1:19)** There is internal harmony within the doctrine of substitutionary atonement that can be seen throughout both the Old and New Testaments.

External harmony looks at consistency across doctrines. Does our teaching in one subject compliment or contradict our teaching in another? Consider the doctrine of "justice" (God's holiness demands that sin be punished). Now consider the doctrine of "mercy" (God forgives sinners). At first, the two doctrines are incompatible. It takes a third doctrine ("substitutionary atonement") to bring them into harmony. The punishment for our sin was paid in full by Christ, thus satisfying God's demand for justice. Since justice has been fully satisfied, God can now extend His mercy and forgiveness to us, the sinners. "He made Him who knew no sin to be sin on our behalf, so that we might become the righteousness of God in Him **(2 Corinthians 5:21)** having forgiven us all our transgressions, having canceled out the certificate of debt consisting of decrees against us, which was hostile to us; and He has taken it out of the way, having nailed it to the cross…" **(Colossians 2:13-14)** Amen for that!

Please understand that doctrinal harmony does not mean doctrinal compromise. Truth is truth because it is true. We are merely identifying those places where the truth is "both/and" versus "either/or." This systematic striving for wholeness produces a more complete theological picture. The sum is greater than its parts. We consider the (singular) Bible to be one complete work even though it is comprised of 66 individual books. Likewise, our individual doctrines should work in harmony together to give us a more complete understanding of God.

Solid theology is based on facts and credible evidence. We start with the facts themselves. By using the Bible, science, archaeology, history, and other credible sources, we gather as much information as we can about the subject in question. Once again, Scripture is our standard. When collecting information, we must be careful to distinguish between fact and fiction. We must also beware of fiction passed on as fact. Slant and repetition are effective elements in both secular and Christian arenas. If a slanted story is repeated long enough, it eventually becomes perceived as fact. Likewise, many "Christianoid" stories that begin as sermon illustrations get passed around in church circles until they are eventually assumed to be true. This is why we as believers must spend the bulk of our reading in the actual Bible rather than in books written about the Bible. Some books can be helpful, but they are not the Bible. Christian fiction may be entertaining, but we do not derive our theology from it.

As a brief exercise in fact finding, let's take a look at **Matthew 27:51**. This passage tells us that when Jesus was crucified, "behold, the veil of the temple was torn in two from top to bottom…" From additional scripture and historical references, we know that the veil is what separated the Holy of Holies (where God was) from the holy place (where man was) **(Exodus 26:33)**. We also know that designs of cherubim were woven into the veil **(Exodus 26:31)**. Similar cherubim were stationed at the Garden of Eden to guard the way to the tree of life after the fall of man **(Genesis 3:24-25)**. Josephus, the famous historian, tells us that the veil in Herod's Temple (the temple at the time of Christ) was woven to be 30 feet wide, 60 feet tall, and 3 inches thick. These are just a few of the facts that can be gathered about this verse and we will refer back to them in a moment.

After fact finding comes "exposition." To exposit simply means "to explain," or "to interpret." Exposition is not just presenting the facts themselves, nor is it simply putting those facts in good order. Instead, exposition tries to explain the practical theological implications of the facts. In other words, how does this information affect our lives? Let's continue with the example from **Matthew 27:51.** First, the veil was "torn." There is no longer a division between the Holy of Holies and the holy place. We now have open access to God through Christ's finished work on the cross. Next, the veil was "30 feet wide, 60 feet tall, and 3 inches thick." No human being is strong enough to tear woven fabric of this magnitude. It is physically impossible, and indicates that this was a miraculous event. Finally, the veil was torn from "top to bottom." If a man tore the veil, it would have been from bottom to top (unless you know of any 60 ft. men). Among other things, the tearing of the veil in this direction serves to show the fundamental difference between religion (our attempt to work our way up to heaven) and true faith in God (our salvation only by God's grace coming down to us).

One of the key ingredients for good systematic theologically is the appreciation of balance. We consider all sides of a doctrinal issue without ignoring the passages that contradict our own personal view. Balance takes into account the whole counsel of God. This is why verse-by-verse Bible study is so essential for us personally and congregationally. We cannot have Biblical balance unless we actually know what's in the Bible - every verse, every chapter, every book. We cannot skip the parts that we don't like, or that make us uncomfortable, or that we simply don't understand. For example, the classic debate over whether or not we can lose our salvation. Passages like **Romans 8:38-39** indicate that we have unconditional salvation (once saved, always saved). On the other hand, passages like **Hebrews 6:4-8** seem to indicate that our salvation is conditional (we can lose it). Remembering our analogy of the cone, balanced harmony comes with a third perspective. In this case, **James 2:14-18**, which basically says,

"Faith works." We are saved unconditionally by faith, but genuine faith shows evidence of itself through our good works. When we understand the balance of scripture, many of the shadowy issues that plague us disappear under the bright light of truth.

Systematic theology also relies on having the right perspective to appreciate specific doctrines in their relation to the bigger picture. The reasoning process is similar to a camera lens zooming in rather than zooming out. We always keep the big picture in mind as we focus in on the details. Imagine taking a photograph of a person's face, then zooming in on the iris of the eye with all of its colors and textures. The magnification may only allow us to view the iris, but we still know that the iris is part of an eye that is part of a face that is part of a person. In other words, we have context. Now, imagine that we are only shown the iris without ever seeing the whole picture. We have no context. We might interpret the object to be part of an eye or perhaps some kind of abstract modern art. Who knows? The same concept is true for studying doctrines. If we don't have the big picture (a "systematic" theology), then we leave ourselves open to focus on one tiny piece of Scripture that we may or may not interpret correctly. As the old saying goes, we won't see the forest for the trees.

Finally, when drawing conclusions through our systematic study of scripture, here are four basic things to keep in mind:

1. **We derive our conclusions from the facts.** Do the facts support what we say we believe? The facts do not change, we do. As believers, we are all in process. As long as we are in this body, not a single one of us can claim to already be "conformed to the image of His Son." **(Romans 8:29)** Not one of us is yet "perfect as (our) heavenly Father is perfect." **(Matthew 5:48)** Therefore, we should not be

surprised that our personal theology is forced to change from time to time to conform to the facts of Scripture. That is simply part of our growing and maturing in Christ. The time to worry is when we think that we have our theology 100% nailed down. Again, only "fools despise wisdom and instruction." **(Proverbs 1:7)**

2. **We build our theology on the clear passages first.** We then try to explain the difficult passages in harmony with the clear ones. Our tendency is to gravitate to the obscure passages, but the reality is that most of the Bible is very straightforward. God means what He says and He says what He means. The few passages that are frequently debated usually deal with non-essentials, yet these are the very topics that generate the most heated arguments. As the saying goes, "The main things are the plain things, and the plain things are the main things." Let us stop arguing about the things that we do not know and start living out the things that we do know. That alone should keep us busy enough for a lifetime.

3. **We honestly acknowledge when we do not have the answers.** This is a difficult lesson for us to learn, especially if we teach. We all want to feel like we've got it all together, but the truth of the matter is that we don't. None of us do. We need to be comfortable saying, "I do not know, but I am seeking the answer." This is a much more legitimate response than our trying to make up something that sounds good in the hope that somehow our answer will save the day. People are not

looking for answers so much as they are looking for the honest truth. Let's at least give them that.

4. **We rely on the Holy Spirit.** "But when He, the Spirit of truth, comes, He will guide you into all the truth; for He will not speak on His own initiative, but whatever He hears, He will speak; and He will disclose to you what is to come. He will glorify Me (Jesus), for He will take of Mine and will disclose it to you." **(John 16:13-14)** And "He will teach you all things, and bring to your remembrance all that I said to you." **(John 14:26)** Let us not forget that the all-knowing God is the One who lives within us. "Now we have received, not the spirit of the world, but the Spirit who is from God, so that we may know the things freely given to us by God, which things we also speak, not in words taught by human wisdom, but in those taught by the Spirit, combining spiritual thoughts with spiritual words. But a natural man does not accept the things of the Spirit of God, for they are foolishness to him; and he cannot understand them, because they are spiritually appraised. But he who is spiritual appraises all things, yet he himself is appraised by no one. For WHO HAS KNOWN THE MIND OF THE LORD, THAT HE WILL INSTRUCT HIM? But we have the mind of Christ." **(1 Corinthians 2:12-16)**

This has been a very brief overview of the basics of systematic theology. For more in depth coverage of specific doctrines, you may want to consider something like **Systematic Theology (4 volume set) by Norman Geisler (ISBN 0764280732).** As always, be "Berean!" **(Acts 17:10-11)**

CHAPTER 6

BIBLE BASICS, PART 6

In this section, we take a look at some practical methods and resources for making our personal Bible study more efficient and effective. Many of these techniques may seem obvious, but growth comes not in the knowing, but in the doing. "The spirit is willing, but the flesh is weak." **(Matthew 26:41)**

BASIC PRINCIPLES. The first basic principle of Bible study is discipline. There are no shortcuts. Our growth is directly proportional to our time alone with God and our time in His Word. "For though by this time you ought to be teachers, you have need again for someone to teach you the elementary principles of the oracles of God, and you have come to need milk and not solid food. For everyone who partakes only of milk is not accustomed to the word of righteousness, for he is an infant. But solid food is for the mature, who *because of practice* have their senses trained to discern good and evil." **(Hebrews 5:12-14)** Jesus said, "Go and make *disciples*." **(Matthew 28:19)** A disciple is much different than a convert. A disciple is disciplined, in preparation for a life-long walk with Christ. As with physical fitness, spiritual fitness requires consistent practice. We cannot expect to win a marathon without training for it; neither should we expect to know the Bible without reading it. "Do you not know that those who run in a race all run, but only one receives the prize? Run in such a way that you may win. Everyone who competes in the games exercises self-control in all things. They then do it to receive a perishable wreath, but we an imperishable. Therefore I run in such a way, as not without aim; I box in such a way, as not beating the air; but I discipline my body and make it my slave, so that, after I have preached to others, I myself will not be disqualified." **(1 Corinthians 9:24-27)** "Bodily discipline is only of little profit, but godliness is profitable for all things, since it holds promise for the present life and also for the life to come." **(1 Timothy 4:8)**

Discipline involves spending actual time in God's Word. If we do not schedule or set aside time to study, it probably will not happen. That is simply the reality of it. The other reality is that the time we set aside should be quality time, whenever we are at our personal physical best. If we are not alert and paying attention when we read, we'll end up missing most of it anyway, so why bother? In Christian circles, "doing devotions" has become a common phrase. However, devotion is something we are, not some thing we do. We must be careful not to adopt a "going-through-the-motions" mentality toward our time in God's Word. We should give God our best, not our leftovers. If that means getting up a little earlier, or going to bed a little later, or skipping a meal, so be it. With God's Word, the return will always outweigh our initial investment, "for momentary, light affliction is producing for us an eternal weight of glory far beyond all comparison, while we look not at the things which are seen, but at the things which are not seen; for the things which are seen are temporal, but the things which are not seen are eternal." **(2 Corinthians 4:17-18)**

Discipline involves prayer. The Word of God is revealed by the God of the Word. We should pray before, during, and after Bible study, asking God to show us what we need to see in His Word. "But if any of you lacks wisdom, let him ask of God, who gives to all generously and without reproach, and it will be given to him." **(James 1:5)**

Finally, discipline involves focus. We need to at least try to remove all possible distractions when we study. That means turning off the phone, the computer, the television, etc. Many of us will even designate a separate, quiet room specifically set aside for Bible study. There is something to be said for solitude. Remember, Bible study is a spiritual battleground in which we are "taking every thought captive to the obedience of Christ." **(2 Corinthians 10:5)** Since it is such a battleground, we can most certainly expect frequent attacks on our quiet time with God. It is almost inevitable that thoughts concerning the business of the day will creep into our minds as we study. We can deal with those random thoughts simply by keeping a pen and paper on hand as we study. We write those thoughts down as they come so we can let them go for now and get back to concentrating on His Word. By the time our study is finished, we usually have a fairly extensive "to do" list that helps us navigate the rest of our day more efficiently. Consider it a bonus for time well spent in the Word.

The second basic principle of Bible study is asking questions. We do not have all the answers, but God does, and He knows us better than we know ourselves. We start with personal questions. What do I know? What do I not know? What do I need to change? For what do I need forgiveness? What do I need to start believing? What do I need to stop believing? These are not superficial, head knowledge questions. These are deeply honest, life application questions. God uses His Word to change us to become more like Himself. This type of change only takes place when we are willing to honestly face the tough questions of life. We are reminded once again, "the word of God is living and active and sharper than any two-edged sword, and piercing as far as the division of soul and spirit, of both joints and marrow, and able to judge the thoughts and intentions of the heart. And there is no creature hidden from His sight, but all things are open and laid bare to the eyes of Him with whom we have to do." **(Hebrews 4:12-13)**

Asking questions within a group requires the same degree of honesty as asking questions of an individual, but many of us find it difficult to be that transparent in public. Still, we must try, and here are two fundamental principles that will help us insure more honest group Bible study:

1. Never ask the group a question that we are not genuinely asking ourselves. We are the ones who have to make the first move. Typical, fill-in-the-blank questions tend to promote what we call "classroom syndrome" (the

subconscious feeling that we are back in school and are about to take a test). We may remain silent, fearing that we may give a wrong answer, or we may simply give a guarded answer that is safe. Either way, we've lost a level of honesty. The whole point of group Bible study is to stretch and challenge us to grow beyond ourselves. The group needs to know that we can be deeply honest with each other without fear of rejection or ridicule. As leaders, we are the ones who promote such an environment by asking only those questions that we are genuinely wrestling with ourselves.

2. Don't be afraid to ask the group a question to which we do not have the answer. "Iron sharpens iron, so one man sharpens another." **(Proverbs 27:17)** If we truly believe that the ground is level at the foot of the cross and that every believer brings something to the table that the rest of us don't have, then we need to frame our questions in such a way as to allow each member the opportunity to minister to each other. Almost without fail, God has brought others into our fellowship who are struggling with the same questions we have. And almost without fail, God has brought others into our fellowship who have already wrestled and have overcome such questions.

The final basic principle of Bible study is application. We must be willing to apply what God teaches us through His Word. We are held accountable for what we know. If we are unwilling to apply what He has already taught us, we really can't expect God to teach us anything new without it becoming just another intellectual pursuit. We must "prove (ourselves) doers of the word, and not merely hearers who delude (ourselves). For if anyone is a hearer of the word and not a doer, he is like a man who looks at his natural face in a mirror; for once he has looked at himself and gone away, he has immediately forgotten what kind of person he was. But one who looks intently at the perfect law, the law of liberty, and abides by it, not having become a forgetful hearer but an effectual doer, this man will be blessed in what he does." **(James 1:22-25)**

Likewise, Jesus said, "Everyone who hears these words of Mine and *acts on them*, may be compared to a wise man who built his house on the rock. And the rain fell, and the floods came, and the winds blew and slammed against that house; and yet it did not fall, for it had been founded on the rock. Everyone who hears these words of Mine and *does not act on them*, will be like a foolish man who built his house on the sand. The rain fell, and the floods came, and the winds blew and slammed against that house; and it fell – and great was its fall." **(Matthew 7:24-27)**

BIBLE STUDY TYPES. There are only two types of Bible study: "Topical" and "Verse-by-Verse" (sometimes referred to as "expositional," meaning, "to explain").

Topical study selects a subject (topic) and traces it through the Bible. Although topical studies contain many subcategories and variations, they are all still topical in nature since they revolve around a specific subject. Topical studies are popular for their convenience since they can easily be tailored to fit specific group interests or time constraints. If done well, topical studies can be very effective and dynamic. However, when done poorly, topical studies can be very dangerous. They are prone to cover only the subjects that hold our interest, and they also tend to be skewed to support our own view or agenda without us even realizing it. This is why it is so important for us to have a well-balanced, systematic approach to Bible study.

Verse-By-Verse study walks through a passage or a book of the Bible in sequence and in context. This is our preferred type of Bible study and we strongly encourage everyone to go this route. There is both safety and challenge in this method. The safety comes from knowing that we are remaining squarely within the boundaries of God's Word. As such, the message will always be effective and relevant. In addition, we never have to worry about what topic to come up with next. If we are in **Matthew chapter 2** this week, we will be in **Matthew chapter 3** next week. Everyone is on the same page. Those who want to can study ahead, and newcomers find it easier to catch up to the group. The challenge comes from the fact that we are working through the "whole counsel of God." **(Acts 20:27)** As such, we are forced to study topics that we may not fully understand or that make us uncomfortable. We cannot just pick what we like. This challenge works to our good by stretching us in areas that we normally would not choose to stretch. It also gives us a more balanced spiritual diet. Verse-by-verse Bible study takes some practice to become proficient, but it can certainly be done and it is certainly worth the effort, both individually and as a congregation.

There are 1,189 chapters in the Bible. If a congregation studies one chapter per week, it would take nearly 23 years to complete. This is a daunting fact, but it should remind us that the best time to start is now. Again, we cannot expect our congregations to know the Bible if we are not committed to teaching it. Realizing that many attempt to read the whole Bible from Genesis thru Revelation only to get bored and quit by the time they get to Leviticus, we have mapped out two refreshing ways to study the Bible in its entirety. As individuals, we read one chapter from the Old Testament at night and one chapter of the New Testament in the morning. As a congregation, we study the books of the Bible alphabetically. This provides some variety to the study as we move between Old and New Testaments and between different types of books.

The alphabetical list of books is as follows: Acts, Amos, 1 Chronicles, 2 Chronicles, Colossians, 1 Corinthians, 2 Corinthians, Daniel, Deuteronomy, Ecclesiastes, Ephesians, Esther, Exodus, Ezekiel, Ezra, Galatians, Genesis, Habakkuk, Haggai, Hebrews, Hosea, Isaiah, James, Job, Joel, John (gospel), 1 John, 2 John, 3 John, Jonah, Joshua, Jude, Judges, 1 Kings, 2 Kings, Lamentations, Leviticus, Luke, Malachi Mark, Matthew, Micah, Nahum, Nehemiah, Numbers, Obadiah, 1 Peter, 2 Peter, Philemon, Philippians, Proverbs, Psalms, Revelation, Romans, Ruth, 1 Samuel, 2 Samuel, Song of Songs (Solomon), 1 Thessalonians, 2 Thessalonians, 1 Timothy, 2 Timothy, Titus, Zechariah, Zephaniah.

BIBLE STUDY METHODS. Sometimes, a different perspective is all it takes to turn an old familiar passage into something brand new. The following are a few simple techniques that can help strengthen and refresh our Bible study:

Repetitive Reading. We refer to this technique as "chewing our food." We start by simply reading a passage and allowing it to soak in. We read the passage at least three times without stopping or writing anything down. We then read through it again, this time paying more attention to detail. Now is the time to write things down. The goal of this technique is to see the big picture and to allow the Bible to speak for itself. We should make a habit of repetitive reading first before we read any commentaries or extra-biblical materials. That way, we keep our perspective clear, and we give the Holy Spirit the opportunity to teach us and to bring things to our remembrance **(John 14:26)** without any prior outside influences.

Word Emphasis. In this technique, we underline different key words in the passage to see how emphasizing each one changes the focus of the message. Word emphasis brings out many new thoughts and questions from what may have become an old, familiar passage. For example, let's look at one small part of **John 3:16**, emphasizing key words as we go:

> "For **God** so loved the world…." God is the One who did it - not ourselves, not Buddha, not Mohammed, etc. - God.

> "For God so **loved** the world…" The motivation is love. The following verse continues, "for God did not send the Son into the world to judge the world, but that the world might be saved through Him." **(John 3:17)** Our motivation for sharing the gospel should be the same as His.

> "For God so loved **the world**…." God loves the entire world, not just one country or a select few.

Salvation is a free and open invitation to all who will receive it.

Repetitive reading and word emphasis are two simple yet extremely effective techniques that require nothing more than our Bible. The power of simply reading the Bible cannot be overstated, especially when we read it together in a group. One thing that we always do at the end of our group Bible study is to ask each person the question, "What did you personally get out of it?" We are always amazed that out of 20 people in the room, all of us reading the same passage together, there will be 20 different yet perfectly on-target answers to that question. The reason is profoundly simple: The Bible is a spiritual book. It speaks to each of us right where we are. We just have to let it speak.

To convince reluctant congregations to get back to basic, verse-by-verse Bible study, we suggest this simple demonstration: Get into groups of four with Bibles open to **Matthew 5:1-12**. Have each person in the group read aloud three verses from this passage. When all have finished, without doing anything more, each person briefly tell the others what part means the most to them from this passage and why. Prepare to be amazed. We have used this exercise with pastors all over the world to demonstrate the fact that we don't need the latest workbooks or multi-media presentations for the Bible to come alive. All we need is what we have always needed: The Holy Spirit, God's Word, and each other. You are the Church.

Summary. In this technique, we write down a brief overview of the entire chapter or book, listing the main sections and ideas in outline form. This is another "big picture" method that helps us preserve the general flow and context of the passages we are studying. A summary is a good place to start before diving into a new verse-by-verse study. **"The Layman's Bible Handbook" (ISBN 1-58660-679-4)** is an excellent resource for summaries.

Biography. Biography is really a topical study where the topic is a person. This method takes an in-depth look at a Bible character as he or she is woven into Scripture. Here, we want to pay particular attention to the person's spiritual strengths and weaknesses. There are over 3,000 people mentioned in the Bible, so we want to be sure that we are researching the correct person since some of the names are shared ("John" could be the apostle, or the Baptist, or John Mark, etc.). Biblical names often had meanings that shed light on a person's character or mission. Changes to those names often signified a change of character or mission. For example, "Abram" (exalted father) was changed to "Abraham" (father of a multitude). The following are good resources for names and biographies: **Nelson's Illustrated Manners and Customs of the Bible (ISBN 07852-5042-5), Nelson's New Illustrated Bible Dictionary (ISBN 0-8407-2071-8), Zondervan Pictoral Encyclopedia of the Bible (ISBN 0-310-33188-9)**.

Historical Background. This technique researches the culture, politics, religious atmosphere, geography, key events, etc. surrounding a book or passage. Essentially, we are preparing to keep the historical context in focus. Most of the resources used in this technique will be outside of the Bible and will be more archaeological in nature. The following are good references for historical background information: **Nelson's Illustrated Manners and Customs of the Bible**

(ISBN 07852-5042-5), Zondervan Pictoral Encyclopedia of the Bible (ISBN 0-310-33188-9).

Word Study. Here, we are taking an in-depth look at the meaning of key words in a passage. Word Study is by far one of the best Bible study techniques we can use and it integrates perfectly into all other methods. When we understand how the Bible is translated into our own language, we realize the value of going back to the original Hebrew, Aramaic, and Greek. Since most of us are not fluent in those original languages, we highly recommend the following resources for Word Study: An <u>exhaustive</u> concordance matched to the translation you study, the **Complete Word Study Dictionary, Old Testament (0-89957-667-2),** and the **Complete Word Study Dictionary, New Testament (0-89957-663-X).**

In word study, we first look at **Definition.** What does the word literally mean in the original language? The Bible contains 11,280 different words in the original Hebrew, Aramaic and Greek. These have been translated into only about 6,000 English words – nearly a 50% reduction! By going back to the original meaning, we can reclaim some of the nuances that may have been lost in translation.

Next, we look at **Roots.** What is the origin of the word? Is there a recurring theme that runs through key words? Many Biblical words, especially in the New Testament, share common roots with words we use today. For example, "spirit" in the New Testament is "pneuma," referring to "air" or "breath," from which we derive words like "pneumonia" or "pneumatic." Sometimes, we begin to see patterns or themes in the original language that we would otherwise miss in our own language.

The book of James, for example, uses a lot of maritime (sailing) terms in the original. These terms smoothly tie verses together which may otherwise have seemed disjointed.

Finally, we look at **Occurrence and Usage**. Where else is the word used? How many times is it used? What is the context of the other Scriptures in which it is used? Asking questions of occurrence and usage leads us to other similar Scriptures. This is the first step in allowing the Bible to be its own best commentary.

RESOURCES. The only book we really need is the Bible. However, some additional resources are helpful for in-depth study if we have access to them and if we can afford them. A lot of money can be spent unnecessarily on books that are not very useful. To spare the disappointment and expense, we have compiled the following list of resources that we have found to be consistently helpful throughout the years. We have listed these in order of importance (what we would buy first) along with a brief explanation of how to use each one. If possible, we strongly recommend that a congregation invest in several copies of these books to keep as a library for those who may not be able to afford them on their own. There are also electronic versions of these resources, many of which are free to the public.

1. **Study Bibles.** Either the **"NIV Hebrew-Greek Key Word Study Bible" (ISBN 0899577008)** or **"Today's Parallel Bible" (ISBN 0310918367)**. If we were to invest in only one Bible, these are our top picks. For the average person looking for an overall study Bible complete with references, go with the Key Word Study Bible. Although we personally prefer the NASB for its accuracy, we usually recommend the NIV for its readability.

For a person wanting a broad spectrum of translations all in one place, go with the Parallel Bible. It has the New American Standard (NASB), King James (KJV), New International (NIV), and New Living (NLT) side-by-side for quick comparison of literal and free translations. It also contains some cross-references, but not many.

2. **"Exhaustive" Concordances.** Either the **"NASB Exhaustive Concordance"** (0-310-26284-4), **"NIV Exhaustive Concordance"** (0-310-26285-2), or **"KJV Strong's Exhaustive Concordance"** (0310233437). James Strong (1822-1894) dedicated his life to the monumental task of cataloguing every Biblical word in the original Hebrew, Aramaic and Greek, assigning a specific number to each word for precise reference and cross-reference. Although originally intended for the King James Version, countless study materials are "keyed" to Strong's numbering system. Other than the Bible itself, we can think of no better book to have on hand than a good concordance.

The two major requirements for a good concordance are that it be **1)** "exhaustive," and **2)** matched to whatever translation we are using for study. "Exhaustive" simply means that it contains every word in the Bible (not a condensed version like many of those found in the backs of most Bibles). Because exhaustive concordances are catalogues of every original word, only those Bibles that are literal, word-for-word translations (NASB, KJV, NKJV, NIV) have matching concordances. Free, thought-for-thought, and paraphrase Bibles do not have matching concordances that are truly exhaustive. It is VERY important to match the concordance with the translation we use because different words are used in different translations. For example, NASB uses "patience", whereas KJV uses "longsuffering." If we study from the NASB and try to look up a "patience" verse in the KJV concordance, we won't find it.

A concordance may look intimidating at first, but it is actually quite easy to use. For example, let's take the word "patience." If we open our concordance to the word "patience" (listed alphabetically), we see a list of Bible verses containing the word. The verses are often given as partial phrases, like "…when the patience of God kept waiting…" to provide us with just enough information to know what verse we are trying to find. Sometimes, the word is represented by its first letter, such as "…when the **p** of God kept waiting…" to save space. Next to the phrase is the Bible reference (in this case, **1 Peter 3:20**). Next to the Bible reference is the Strong's number for that specific word as it appears in the original language (in this case, 3115). We notice that there are different Strong's numbers listed for different verses (3115, 750, 3811, 3114, 5278, etc.). This is because several different original words have all been translated into our one English word, "patience" (remember, 11,280 original words have been reduced to 6,000 English words).

In the back of most exhaustive concordances we find Hebrew and Greek dictionaries. Typically, these are not very helpful, but they do give the spelling and origin of the word. To use the dictionary section, take the Strong's number of the word we are working with and find it listed numerically in either the Old Testament (Hebrew) dictionary or in the New Testament (Greek) dictionary. The numbering is different for Old and New Testaments, so keep that in mind when cross-referencing verses from different Testaments.

One word of caution regarding the NIV exhaustive concordance. The NIV uses the Goodrick-Kohlenberger (GK) numbering system rather than the Strong's numbering system. So, in order to find the Strong's number in the NIV concordance, we have to go to the back section and find a "conversion chart" that goes from GK to Strong's and from Strong's to GK. This is an annoying extra step that can be discouraging when using the NIV for study since so many other references are already keyed directly to the Strong's numbers without having to convert.

3. **Hebrew and Greek Dictionaries.** We definitely recommend both the **"Complete Word Study Dictionary, Old Testament" (0-89957-667-2)** and **"Complete Word Study Dictionary, New Testament" (0-89957-663-X).** For understanding what the original word actually means, we cannot speak more highly of these Word Study Dictionaries. The Key Word Study Bible contains some of this information, but the separate dictionaries are much more complete in their descriptions and cross-references. They are keyed directly to Strong's numbers for easy reference. We simply look

up the word in our concordance, get the number, then go to that number in either the Old or New Testament Word Study Dictionary for the full explanation.

4. **Bible Dictionaries.** The **"Nelson's New Illustrated Bible Dictionary" (0-8407-2071-8).** This book is a cross between an encyclopedia and a dictionary. It has great photos and illustrations, and it proves to be a quick reference for many Biblical, cultural, and historical subjects. For those who really enjoy reading, this is a book that is interesting enough to read cover-to-cover as it contains a lot of helpful and enlightening material that we might not have looked up intentionally.

5. **Bible Encyclopedias.** The **"Zondervan Pictoral Encyclopedia of the Bible" (5 volumes)(0-310-33188-9)** and **"Nelson's Illustrated Manners and Customs of the Bible" (07852-5042-5).** Similar to Bible dictionaries, the encyclopedias give insight into Biblical culture and history but with greater detail. The Pictoral, multi-volume set is definitely sufficient, but the Manners and Customs book contains a lot of older, "lost" material that helps to fill in some of the gaps, especially when it comes to the names of people and places.

6. **Handbooks.** The **"Layman's Bible Handbook" (1-58660-679-4).** This convenient little book serves as an excellent summary of Biblical content. There are other Bible handbooks available (Halley's, etc.), but those function more like condensed Bible

encyclopedias rather than as dedicated summaries. The Layman's Handbook is particularly effective when used as the basis for Old & New Testament surveys.

7. **Commentaries.** The **"Expositor's Bible Commentary (Abridged Edition), Old Testament"** (0-310-25496-5) and **"Expositor's Bible Commentary (Abridged Edition), New Testament"** (0-310-25497-3). Commentaries should be our very last resort. They are no substitute for solid, personal Bible study. Commentary is just that - "commentary" (running remarks written by fallible men and women to the best of their ability). There are literally hundreds of them available depending on our taste. Some commentaries cover the entire Bible while others cover a single book. When choosing commentaries, we want to look for those that have been written by a panel of authors rather than by a single author. This keeps things more balanced and less prone to wildly straying opinion. We like the Expositor's Commentary for its factual and neutral presentation. Although there is an unabridged (12 volume) set, we prefer the abridged (2-volume) edition because it contains all of the essential material without dwelling on as many grammatical details which can be quite tedious to read.

8. **Bookstores.** **"Christian Book Distributors"** (CBD) (www.christianbook.com) and **"Amazon"** (www.amazon.com). These two stores tend to have the best prices and selection for Christian reference books.

9. **Electronic Bible References.** **"E-sword"** (www.e-sword.net), **"Bible Gateway"** (www.biblegateway.com), **"Crosswalk"** (www.crosswalk.com), **"Olive Tree"** (www.olivetree.com), and **"Logos"** (www.logos.com). "E-sword" is an excellent software program that is completely FREE. The best part is that it downloads directly to our computer so we don't have to be online to use it. The program offers many free Bibles, dictionaries, commentaries, etc., and they are all integrated together. Additional references (including most of the books mentioned above) can be purchased as integrated, fully-compatible downloads for "E-sword." We can even add our own personal notes and observations to the program, and those become integrated as well. "Bible Gateway" and "Crosswalk" function much like "E-sword," but we have to be online to use them. "Olive Tree" offers many downloads for PDA's and smart phones if portability is an issue. "Logos" is the most comprehensive, featuring online and offline material compatible with desktop computers, tablets, or smartphones. The major drawback is price – Logos can be quite expensive.

Now that we have a basic understanding of the Bible and how to study it, the only thing holding us back is our own motivation. With a bit of discipline and a few good resources, there are no excuses for any of us not to grow stronger in God's Word. The question is whether or not we will put in the time and effort to do it.

CHAPTER 7

FELLOWSHIP

There is perhaps no greater statement regarding Christian fellowship than that which was made by Christ Himself: "For where two or three have gathered together in My name, I am there in their midst." **(Matthew 18:20)** We are instructed not to "forsake our own assembling together" **(Hebrews 10:25)** for in some profound, divinely inexplicable way, as we come into the presence of our brethren, we come into the presence of God. However, true Christian fellowship differs greatly from mere social interaction. It is more intentional, genuine, and purposeful. Biblical fellowship is practiced through authentic relationships and service. It is something that must be experienced rather than explained.

Let us be perfectly clear that "going to church on Sunday" is not the Biblical requirement or definition of fellowship. The truth is, fellowship occurs whenever and wherever "two or three have gathered in (His) name." Size and/or formality have nothing to do with it. When referring to fellowship, the Bible uses the Greek word "koinonia," meaning "mutual participation, community, and intimacy." In short, it means sharing life together through mutual encouragement, support, accountability, and service. Consistent fellowship with other believers is a vital and necessary part of our own personal spiritual growth. Fellowship is essential for the building up of the body of Christ and none of us can (nor should) go it alone.

So what makes Christian fellowship unique? In other words, how is it really any different from any other social gathering or organization? First, koinonia is Christ-centered. Through our faith, we have fellowship with:

1. **Jesus.** "God is faithful, through whom you were called into fellowship with His Son, Jesus Christ our Lord." **(1 Corinthians 1:9)** Our personal relationship with Jesus is the fundamental basis for all Christian fellowship. There are no Christians without the Christ.

2. **The Father.** "Jesus answered and said to him, 'If anyone loves Me, he will keep My word; and My Father will love him, and We will come to him and make Our abode with him.'" **(John 14:23)** We cannot bypass Jesus to get to God. Our relationship with the Father comes only through the Son. "Jesus said to (Thomas), 'I am the way, and the truth, and the life; no one comes to the Father but through Me.'" **(John 14:6)** "He who

has the Son has the life; he who does not have the Son of God does not have the life." **(1 John 5:12)**

3. **Other Believers.** "What we have seen and heard we proclaim to you also, so that you too may have fellowship with us; and indeed our fellowship is with the Father, and with His Son Jesus Christ." **(1 John 1:3)** Our common bond of faith in Christ is that which forms our common foundation and sets us on a common path toward a common goal. "There is one body and one Spirit, just as also you were called in one hope of your calling; one Lord, one faith, one baptism, one God and Father of all who is over all and through all and in all." **(Ephesians 4:4-6)** Although we may have relationships with unbelievers (even deep, meaningful ones), they are never the same as the fellowship experienced between believers. We are instructed "not to be bound together with unbelievers; for what partnership have righteousness and lawlessness, or what fellowship has light with darkness?" **(2 Corinthians 6:14)** This is not to exclude our contact with our unbelieving friends, but it is certainly to exclude our being "bound together" with them. There is a difference. "Do not be deceived: 'bad company corrupts good morals." **(1 Corinthians 15:33)**

Second, koinonia is purposeful. Fellowship sets higher goals than we could set for ourselves alone. Through true Christian fellowship, we experience:

1. **Belonging.** We are part of something bigger than ourselves. "So we, who are many, are one body in Christ, and individually members one of another." **(Romans 12:5)** "And if one member suffers, all the members suffer with it; if one member is honored, all the members rejoice with it." **(1 Corinthians 12:26)**

2. **Encouragement.** We help each other realize our potential in Christ. "Realization" encompasses not only the discovery or acknowledgement of one's potential, but the actual achievement of it as well. We are taught to "consider how to stimulate one another to love and good deeds, not forsaking our own assembling together, as is the habit of some, but encouraging one another; and all the more as (we) see the day drawing near." **(Hebrews 10:24-25)** "Iron sharpens iron, so one man sharpens another." **(Proverbs 27:17)**

3. **Support.** We help each other in time of need. "Two are better than one because they have a good return for their labor. For if either of them falls, the one will lift up his companion. But woe to the one who falls when there is not another to lift him up. Furthermore, if two lie down together they keep warm, but how can one be warm alone? And if one can overpower him who is alone, two can resist him. A cord of three strands is not quickly torn apart." **(Ecclesiastes 4:9-12)**

We are to "bear one another's burdens, and thereby fulfill the law of Christ." **(Galatians 6:2)** In the same passage, we are instructed that "each one will bear his own load." **(Galatians 6:5)** A "load" ('phortion') is the normal weight that each one of us is called to carry in our own service and walk with Christ. A "burden" ('baros'), however, is an extra-heavy weight that we cannot shoulder alone. The balance lies in knowing which is which. This applies to the one bearing the weight and to those who face the decision of whether or not to help. Loads and burdens are not just financial. They can be spiritual, social, emotional, etc. We must be careful not to encourage freeloading, while at the same time, we must be willing to lend a hand to those who truly need it.

This may be an appropriate time to address how giving should be conducted within the Church. It all starts with the teaching of the doctrine of personal financial accountability (good stewardship). God expects each of us to manage well the money and resources that He has entrusted to us personally as individuals. We are instructed "to make it (our) ambition to lead a quiet life and attend to (our) own business and work with (our) hands, just as commanded, so that (we) will behave properly toward outsiders and not be in any need" **(1 Thessalonians 4:10-12)**, and that "if anyone is not willing to work, then he is not to eat, either." **(2 Thessalonians 3:10)** The only way that we can know whether or not a person is willing to work is when we know that person on an intimate level. This kind of knowledge only comes from meeting together in smaller groups where we get to know each other well enough to understand who among us is truly in need and who is not. The traditional model of congregational tithing to a large, organized religious structure to maintain its facilities and programs is not taught in the New Testament. What is taught is personal stewardship and personal commitment to give to those in need. This can only happen when God's people are committed to practicing personal financial accountability. We cannot give if we have nothing to give. And we will not have anything to give until we become good stewards of what we already have. If we allow ourselves to live beyond our means, to become saddled with debt, and to indulge ourselves in lifestyles of fulfilling selfish wants, we become worldly-minded, lose our vision for Kingdom living, and render ourselves ineffective in our ability to help others. Even the former freeloader is instructed to "steal no longer; but rather he must labor, performing with his own hands what is good, so that he will have something to share with one who has need." **(Ephesians 4:28)**

As previously stated (Chapter 3), tithing is an Old Testament law that is not renewed in the New Testament. It is not prohibited, but it's not mandated either. We are free to give as God leads us to give. For those who would argue otherwise, the Biblical example seen in **1 Corinthians 16:1-2** presents a response to a specific need (the famine in Judea **(Acts 11:27-30, Romans 15:25-28)**) rather than a model for tithing to a local church. Yes, we should contribute financially to our local church in some capacity. However, in keeping more consistent with the Biblical context, rather than exclusively giving to a local church organization, we suggest that each individual creates his/her own additional benevolence fund (we call ours the "God fund"). This fund consists of personal finances set aside for the specific purpose of helping others, and the money is not to be used unless God directs the individual to meet a specific need. As a result, the fund may grow, sometimes to large amounts, allowing us to give more abundantly when a need does arise. In this way, we are able to live in a state of readiness to give as God directs. We become personally active in seeking opportunities to meet the needs of others, and we become personally connected in our giving, just as God intended us to be.

4. **Accountability.** We hold each other to a higher standard in Christ. "Brethren, even if anyone is caught in any trespass, you who are spiritual, restore such a one in a spirit of gentleness; each one looking to yourself, so that you too will not be tempted." **(Galatians 6:1)** "My brethren, if any among you strays from the truth and one turns him back, let him know that he who turns a sinner from the error of his way will save his soul from death and will cover a multitude of sins." **(James 5:19-20)** As Christians, we give our brothers and sisters the divine right to interfere in our lives from time to time for our own good. We rely on the objectivity of those who love us enough to show us our blind spots and to help us raise the bar on the spiritual quality of our lives. The parable of the speck and the log **(Matthew 7:1-5)** does not end with our "removing the log that is

in our own eye," but rather continues, "so that we may see clearly to remove the speck that is in our brother's eye." Let us not be so afraid of "judging others lest we be judged" that we neglect to discern and intervene when a brother or sister is in need of correction.

5. **Love.** Our unity and love for each other shows the world that God is real. Jesus said, "A new commandment I give to you, that you love one another, even as I have loved you, that you also love one another. By this all men will know that you are My disciples, if you have love for one another." **(John 13:35)**

All Christian fellowship should exhibit certain fundamental characteristics if it is to be effective. First, we must be committed to sharing life together in a very real and tangible way. The early Church "who had believed were together and had all things in common; and they began selling their property and possessions and were sharing them with all, as anyone might have need. Day by day continuing with one mind in the temple, and breaking bread from house to house, they were taking their meals together with gladness and sincerity of heart." **(Acts 2:44-46)** We need to ask ourselves the question, "Are these people truly our friends and family?" Do we get together and share meals with each other on a regular basis? Do we share good times, bad times, family moments, or holidays with each other? Would we let each other borrow our money or our most prized possessions? Could we spend a month in each other's homes if we have to? If any of these questions make us uncomfortable, then we still have some room to grow in our concept of fellowship.

Second, we need to be completely honest with God, with ourselves, and with each other, especially when it comes to our transparent confession of sin. "What we have seen and heard we proclaim to you also, so that you too may have fellowship with us; and indeed our fellowship is with the Father, and with His Son Jesus Christ. These things we write, so that our joy may be made complete. This is the message we have heard from Him and announce to you, that God is Light, and in Him there is no darkness at all. If we say that we have fellowship with Him and yet walk in the darkness, we lie and do not practice the truth; but if we walk in the Light as He Himself is in the Light, we have fellowship with one another, and the blood of Jesus His Son cleanses us from all sin. If we say that we have no sin, we are deceiving ourselves and the truth is not in us. If we confess our sins, He is faithful and righteous to forgive us our sins and to cleanse us from all unrighteousness." **(1 John 1:3-9)** "Therefore, confess your sins to one another…" **(James 5:16)** Being open enough to confess our sin to each other requires a great deal of trust. To break that trust is to violate the very body of Christ. There is absolutely no room for gossip of any kind. What is said within the fellowship stays within the fellowship.

Third, Christian fellowship involves sacrificial service to one another. "As each one has received a special gift, employ it in serving one another as good stewards of the manifold grace of God. Whoever speaks, is to do so as one who is speaking the utterances of God; whoever serves is to do so as one who is serving by the strength which God supplies; so that in all things God may be glorified through Jesus Christ, to whom belongs the glory and dominion forever and ever.

Amen." **(1 Peter 4:10-11)** "So then, while we have opportunity, let us do good to all people, and especially to those who are of the household of the faith." **(Galatians 6:10)**

On a final note, there is an appropriate time for us to discontinue fellowship with another believer in the exercise of Church discipline. This is a necessary function within the body of Christ and we cannot afford to be neutral or complacent about it. Church discipline must be conducted Biblically and with a great deal of prayer. Our motivation should always be out of love, and our goal should always be for the reconciliation of the backslider. The Bible lays down very clear guidelines for the exercise of Church discipline. Jesus said, "If your brother sins, go and show him his fault in private; if he listens to you, you have won your brother. But if he does not listen to you, take one or two more with you, so that by the mouth of two or three witnesses every fact may be confirmed. If he refuses to listen to them, tell it to the church; and if he refuses to listen even to the church, let him be to you as a Gentile and a tax collector." **(Matthew 18:15-17)** Paul reinforced this teaching by instructing us "not to associate with any so-called brother if he is an immoral person, or covetous, or an idolater, or a reviler, or a swindler – not even to eat with such a one…Do you not judge those who are within the church?…Remove the wicked man from among yourselves." **(1 Corinthians 5:11-13)** Church discipline is never comfortable, but it does have positive results. When the backslidden brother or sister shows genuine repentance, then we must show them genuine forgiveness and welcome them back into fellowship.

"My brethren, if any among you strays from the truth and one turns him back, let him know that he who turns a sinner from the error of his way will save his soul from death and will cover a multitude of sins." **(James 5:19-20)**

CHAPTER 8

COMMUNION

The Church has been given two symbolic observances in the New Testament: Baptism and Communion. Both represent key elements of our faith, and both have been practiced throughout the world since the beginning of Christianity. Baptism is a one-time event that marks the beginning of our new life in Christ. Communion, on the other hand, is an ongoing practice that commemorates our unity as believers through His death, resurrection, and return. Although the frequency and style of the observance may vary, most of us are familiar with some form of communion service as practiced in larger congregations. However, communion is not limited to such formal services nor is it limited to larger organizational gatherings. In this chapter, we will address the basic principles that apply to observing communion in any setting.

Some denominations refer to communion as the "eucharist," a Greek word meaning, "giving thanks." The term comes from **Matthew 26:27** ("And when He had taken a cup and given thanks, He gave it to them…"). Also called the "Lord's Supper," communion literally means, "to hold in common." It is a symbolic memorial that represents the sacrifice of Jesus on our behalf. Through His death and resurrection, we are forgiven of our sin. This commonality (the sharing in the body and blood of Christ) is what brings us into a relationship with God and with other believers. We "hold in common" a shared life in Christ. "Is not the cup of blessing which we bless a sharing in the blood of Christ? Is not the bread which we break a sharing in the body of Christ? Since there is one bread, we who are many are one body; for we all partake of the one bread." **(1 Corinthians 10:16-17)**

The Biblical roots of communion are traced to the Old Testament Passover, a mandatory yearly feast commemorating the freeing of Israel from slavery in Egypt when the angel of death "passed over" the homes that had the blood of the lamb on their doorposts. **(Exodus 11,12)** "…For Christ our Passover also has been sacrificed. Let us therefore celebrate the feast…" **(1 Corinthians 5:7-8)** The New Testament "Last Supper" was the Passover meal that was celebrated by Jesus and His disciples before He was crucified. This was essentially the first Christian communion service. "When the hour had come, He reclined at the table, and the apostles with Him. And He said to them, "I have earnestly desired to eat this Passover with you before I suffer; for I say to you, I shall never again eat it until it is fulfilled in the kingdom of God."" **(Luke 22:14-16)** Interestingly, God never gave the Jews a specific format for how to observe the Passover meal, only the command that they should observe it. During the Last Supper, Jesus took the liberty to alter some of the symbols of the traditional Passover Seder. He did this to demonstrate how He is the ultimate fulfillment of the celebration. These alterations became the foundation for our Christian communion.

We practice communion to remember Jesus. "For I received from the Lord that which I also delivered to you, that the Lord Jesus in the night in which He was betrayed took bread; and when He had given thanks, He broke it and said, "This is My body, which is for you; do this in remembrance of Me." In the same way He took the cup also after supper, saying, "This cup is the new covenant in My blood; do this, as often as you drink it, in remembrance of Me." For as often as you eat this bread and drink the cup, you proclaim the Lord's death until He comes." **(1 Corinthians 11:23-26)** There are no specific guidelines as to how frequently we should observe communion. Jesus simply said, "as often as" you do this. Some congregations have weekly communion, while others observe it annually. We personally have found that quarterly observances work well, especially in our home fellowships.

We also practice communion to examine ourselves. "Therefore whoever eats the bread or drinks the cup of the Lord in an unworthy manner shall be guilty of the body and the blood of the Lord. But a man must examine himself, and in so doing he is to eat of the bread and drink of the cup. For he who eats and drinks, eats and drinks judgment to himself if he does not judge the body rightly. For this reason many among you are weak and sick, and a number sleep. But if we judged ourselves rightly, we would not be judged. But when we are judged, we are disciplined by the Lord so that we will not be condemned along with the world." **(1 Corinthians 11:27-32)** There is a balance between grace and self-examination. On the one hand, the communion table is open to all who are worthy. On the other hand, the communion table is open to all who are worthy. Between the 1500s and the 1800s, believers were so concerned about the qualifications for participating in communion that many churches issued their own communion "tokens" (actual, minted coins that admitted a person into the communion service based on an interview with the pastor). Although we can easily point out the legalism of that approach in light of God's grace, it does beg the question of how seriously (or not) we take self-examination before communion in our churches today.

As a basic guideline, communion should be observed with:

1. **Sincerity.** Communion should be genuine and meaningful as we remember both the holiness and loving kindness of God.

2. **Serenity.** Communion should take place in an environment where we can pray quietly, confess our sin, and reflect on God without distraction. Children are welcome, but each parent should determine which of their children are mature enough to participate in communion with the adults without becoming a distraction.

3. **Simplicity.** All we need is some bread, some grape juice, and some cups. In consideration of our brothers and sisters in Christ, we recommend not serving alcohol at our communion services.

4. **Unity.** In the Biblical culture of the New Testament, bread was the staple food and communions were more like meals (the "love feasts" referred to in **Jude 1:12**). As more and more people began to partake of the free provisions, there was a tendency for gluttony on the part of some at the expense of others (not the kind of unity we would hope for among believers). Nowadays, communion is more of a symbol than a meal, but we must still strive for spiritual unity as we partake of the elements together. We are reminded, "Whenever you stand praying, forgive, if you have anything against anyone, so that your Father who is in heaven will also forgive you your transgressions." **(Mark 11:25)** Likewise, "if you are presenting your offering at the altar, and there remember that your brother has something against you, leave your offering there before the altar and go; first be reconciled to your brother, and then come and present your offering." **(Matthew 5:23-24)** Paul warned the Church at Corinth, "You come together not for the better but for the worse. For, in the first place, when you come together as a church, I hear that divisions exist among you; and in part I believe it. For there must also be factions among you, so that those who are approved may become evident among you. Therefore when you meet together, it is not to eat

the Lord's Supper, for in your eating each one takes his own supper first; and one is hungry and another is drunk. What! Do you not have houses in which to eat and drink? Or do you despise the church of God and shame those who have nothing? What shall I say to you? Shall I praise you? In this I will not praise you... So then, my brethren, when you come together to eat, wait for one another. If anyone is hungry, let him eat at home, so that you will not come together for judgment." **(1 Corinthians 11:17-22, 33-34)**

Although it is a serious observance, communion does not have to be formal, somber, or complicated. The following is a basic outline for a simple communion that can be observed in any setting (as a family, as a home fellowship, or as a larger congregation). This observance takes only about 10-15 minutes:

1. **Someone read the following out loud:** "For I received from the Lord that which I also delivered to you, that the Lord Jesus in the night in which He was betrayed took bread; and when He had given thanks, He broke it and said, "This is My body, which is for you; do this in remembrance of Me." In the same way He took the cup also after supper, saying, "This cup is the new covenant in My blood; do this, as often as you drink it, in remembrance of Me." For as often as you eat this bread and drink the cup, you proclaim the Lord's death until He comes. Therefore whoever eats the bread or drinks the cup of the Lord in an unworthy manner shall be guilty of the body and the blood of the Lord. But a man must examine himself, and in so doing he is to eat of the

bread and drink of the cup. For he who eats and drinks, eats and drinks judgment to himself if he does not judge the body rightly. For this reason many among you are weak and sick, and a number sleep. But if we judged ourselves rightly, we would not be judged. But when we are judged, we are disciplined by the Lord so that we will not be condemned along with the world. So then, my brethren, when you come together to eat, wait for one another. If anyone is hungry, let him eat at home, so that you will not come together for judgment…" **(1 Corinthians 11:23-34)**

2. **Someone open in prayer**. Thank God for what He has done for us through Christ.

3. **Someone break the bread**. Pass the bread around the room, each person taking a piece. Instruct everyone to hold onto the bread and the juice until all have received and after each one has examined himself/herself in prayer.

4. **Someone pour the juice**. Pass the juice around the room, each person taking a cup. Again, instruct everyone to hold onto the bread and the juice until all have received and after each one has examined himself/herself in prayer.

5. **Pray individually together**. Each of us should examine ourselves in prayer, confessing our sin and asking forgiveness. This may be done silently or out loud

depending on the Spirit's leading. The hope is that we will continue to pray and confess more openly with each other, for it is within this context that James wrote for us to "confess (our) sins to one another, and pray for one another so that (we) may be healed..." **(James 5:16)**

6. **Eat the bread and drink the juice.** Each person determines individually when to do this after he/she has had time to set his/her heart right with God.

7. **Someone close in prayer.**

Communion is perhaps the most neglected of the four foundational Church disciplines. Hopefully, this chapter has encouraged us to observe communion more often and with greater significance as we gather together to remember that, "we were not redeemed with perishable things like silver or gold...but with precious blood, as of a lamb unblemished and spotless, the blood of Christ." **(1 Peter 1 18-19)**

CHAPTER 9

PRAYER

Good communication is the key to any strong relationship. Naturally, the strength of our relationship with God is directly related to the quality and consistency of our communication with Him (our prayer life). The goal of this chapter is to understand the basics of prayer so we can incorporate it more effectively into our personal lives. What we are in public should reflect what we are in private. Strong individual prayer lives at home raise the quality of our prayer life together as the Church.

In essence, prayer is a personal, two-way conversation with our heavenly Father. "Because (we) are sons, God has sent forth the Spirit of His Son into our hearts, crying, 'Abba! Father!'"

(Galatians 4:6) The phrase "Abba Father" (Dad) reflects the proper balance between affection and respect. God is at the same time both holy and intimate. Our respect for God should be with affection and our affection for God should be with respect. To fall short of either is to fall short of both.

Fasting is often mentioned together with prayer **(Nehemiah 1:4; Daniel 9:3; Matthew 17:21; Luke 2:37; Acts 14:23, etc.)**, and often within the context of praying over a specific issue of concern. To "fast" is to willingly abstain from something for a period of time. Though most often involving food, fasting can involve anything. By denying our physical desires from time to time, we can train ourselves to focus more intently on spiritual things. Jesus taught, "Whenever you fast, do not put on a gloomy face as the hypocrites do, for they neglect their appearance so that they will be noticed by men when they are fasting. Truly I say to you, they have their reward in full. But you, when you fast, anoint your head and wash your face so that your fasting will not be noticed by men, but by your Father who is in secret; and your Father who sees what is done in secret will reward you." **(Matthew 6:16-18)** Though it requires discipline, fasting should become a consistent and integral part of our prayer lives.

Prayer is so vital to our spiritual health that we are told to "pray without ceasing." **(1 Thessalonians 5:17)** But how should we pray? The early disciples had the same question. "It happened that while Jesus was praying in a certain place, after He had finished, one of His disciples said to Him, 'Lord, teach us to pray just as John also taught his disciples.'" **(Luke 11:1)** To which Jesus responded, "Pray, then, in this way: 'Our

Father who is in heaven, hallowed be Your name. Your kingdom come. Your will be done, On earth as it is in heaven. Give us this day our daily bread. And forgive us our debts, as we also have forgiven our debtors. And do not lead us into temptation, but deliver us from evil. For Yours is the kingdom and the power and the glory forever. Amen.'" **(Matthew 6:9-13)** On a side note, the word "amen" that often closes prayer simply means, "to be firm, steady, or truthful." It's like saying, "let it be for certain" or "so be it."

Jesus taught us how to pray, not what to pray. He gave us an example, not a ritual. The two preceding verses make that perfectly clear when Jesus Himself says, "And when you are praying, do not use meaningless repetition as the Gentiles do, for they suppose that they will be heard for their many words. So do not be like them; for your Father knows what you need before you ask Him." **(Matthew 6:7-8)** Sadly ironic, Jesus' prayer from **Matthew 6** is the most ritually repeated prayer in Church history. While being careful not to fall into the same trap, we do want to highlight some of the key elements found in that particular prayer:

1. **It is to the right God.** Addressing God as "our Father" assumes that we know Him and that we have a personal relationship with Him.

2. **It puts God in His rightful place.** He is "in heaven, hallowed (holy, respected)."

3. **It puts us in our rightful place.** We are totally dependent on God for "our daily bread," for our forgiveness, and for our deliverance.

4. It acknowledges God's sovereignty. "For (His) is the kingdom and the power and the glory forever." He is supremely worthy and able.

Prayer is sincere. We have to be completely honest with God, with ourselves, and with each other. Anything less is hypocrisy (pretending to be what we are not). Let us remember that, "there is no creature hidden from (God's) sight, but all things are open and laid bare to the eyes of Him with whom we have to do." **(Hebrews 4:13)** "There is nothing covered up that will not be revealed, and hidden that will not be known. Accordingly, whatever (we) have said in the dark will be heard in the light, and what (we) have whispered in the inner rooms will be proclaimed upon the housetops." **(Luke 12:2-3)**

Prayer is humble. Jesus said, "When you pray, you are not to be like the hypocrites; for they love to stand and pray in the synagogues and on the street corners so that they may be seen by men. Truly I say to you, they have their reward in full. But you, when you pray, go into your inner room, close your door and pray to your Father who is in secret, and your Father who sees what is done in secret will reward you." **(Matthew 6:5-6)** "And He also told this parable to some people who trusted in themselves that they were righteous, and viewed others with contempt: 'Two men went up into the temple to pray, one a Pharisee and the other a tax collector. The Pharisee stood and was praying this to himself: "God, I thank You that I am not like other people: swindlers, unjust, adulterers, or even like this tax collector. I fast twice a week; I pay tithes of all that I get." But the tax collector, standing some distance away, was even unwilling to lift up his eyes to heaven, but was beating his breast, saying, "God, be merciful to me, the sinner!" 'I tell you, this man went to his house justified rather than the other; for everyone who exalts himself will be humbled, but he who humbles himself will be exalted.'" **(Luke 18:9-14)**

Prayer is thankful. We are to "devote (ourselves) to prayer, keeping alert in it with an attitude of thanksgiving" **(Colossians 4:2)**, and "in everything by prayer and supplication with thanksgiving let (our) requests be made known to God." (**Philippians 4:6**) Our thankfulness expresses gratitude for who God is and for what He has already done. It is an attitude that comes from understanding that God is good; not simply that God does good things, but that He Himself is the very definition of "good." **(Mark 10:18)**

Prayer is confident. Such confidence comes from knowing that God genuinely understands and personally cares about us and about our lives. "For we do not have a high priest who cannot sympathize with our weaknesses, but One who has been tempted in all things as we are, yet without sin. Therefore let us draw near with confidence to the throne of grace, so that we may receive mercy and find grace to help in time of need." **(Hebrews 4:15-16)**

Prayer is persistent. We ask until God answers. However, God is not obligated to answer us according to our own desires or deadlines. Answers can take many forms (yes, no, wait, etc.) and we have to trust that He knows exactly what we need and when we need it. Jesus "was telling (his disciples) a parable to show that at all times they ought to pray and not to lose heart, saying, 'In a certain city there was a judge who did not fear God and did not respect man. There was a widow in that city, and she kept coming to him, saying, "Give me legal protection from my opponent." For a while he was unwilling;

but afterward he said to himself, "Even though I do not fear God nor respect man, yet because this widow bothers me, I will give her legal protection, otherwise by continually coming she will wear me out.'" And the Lord said, 'Hear what the unrighteous judge said; now, will not God bring about justice for His elect who cry to Him day and night, and will He delay long over them? I tell you that He will bring about justice for them quickly. However, when the Son of Man comes, will He find faith on the earth?'" **(Luke 18:1-8)** A sermon for another time perhaps, but it is worth noting that this parable ends with the question of our faith. God will do His part. Will we do ours?

"Then (Jesus) said to them, 'Suppose one of you has a friend, and goes to him at midnight and says to him, "Friend, lend me three loaves; for a friend of mine has come to me from a journey, and I have nothing to set before him"; and from inside he answers and says, "Do not bother me; the door has already been shut and my children and I are in bed; I cannot get up and give you anything." I tell you, even though he will not get up and give him anything because he is his friend, yet because of his persistence he will get up and give him as much as he needs. So I say to you, ask, and it will be given to you; seek, and you will find; knock, and it will be opened to you. For everyone who asks, receives; and he who seeks, finds; and to him who knocks, it will be opened. Now suppose one of you fathers is asked by his son for a fish; he will not give him a snake instead of a fish, will he? Or if he is asked for an egg, he will not give him a scorpion, will he? If you then, being evil, know how to give good gifts to your children, how much more will your heavenly Father give the Holy Spirit to those who ask Him?'" **(Luke 11:5-12)** The verb tense is, "continue to ask;

continue to seek; continue to knock." It is perfectly acceptable for us to ask God for something more than once (**Matthew 6:7-8** is a prohibition against mindless repetition, not against persistent prayer). Paul wrote, "Concerning this (thorn in the flesh) I implored the Lord three times that it might leave me. And He has said to me, 'My grace is sufficient for you, for power is perfected in weakness.' Most gladly, therefore, I will rather boast about my weaknesses, so that the power of Christ may dwell in me." **(2 Corinthians 12:8-9)** That may not have been the answer Paul wanted to hear (even though he asked three times), but it was certainly the answer he needed, when he needed it. It is often only in retrospect that we learn to appreciate God's perfect timing. **(Romans 8:28)**

Prayer is pure. Our motive is to advance God's kingdom, not our own. Otherwise, "(we) lust and do not have; so (we) commit murder. (We) are envious and cannot obtain; so (we) fight and quarrel. (We) do not have because (we) do not ask. (We) ask and do not receive, because (we) ask with wrong motives, so that (we) may spend it on (our) pleasures." **(James 4:2-3)**

Prayer is powerful. It has results. "The effective prayer of a righteous man can accomplish much. Elijah was a man with a nature like ours, and he prayed earnestly that it would not rain, and it did not rain on the earth for three years and six months. Then he prayed again, and the sky poured rain and the earth produced its fruit." **(James 5:16-18)** "But (we) must ask in faith without any doubting, for the one who doubts is like the surf of the sea, driven and tossed by the wind. For that man ought not to expect that he will receive anything from the Lord, being a double-minded man, unstable in all his ways." **(James 1:6-8)** Jesus said, "Truly I say to you, if you have faith and do not doubt…even if you say to this mountain, 'Be taken up and cast into the sea,' it will happen. And all things you ask in prayer, believing, you will receive." **(Matthew 21:18-22)** Given how prone these passages are to blatant abuses, we do well to remember that God is not our servant. He is not obligated to us in any way, whether by positive confession or by any other spiritual gymnastics designed to conjure up enough faith to produce favorable results. Our instruction is to have faith in God, not faith in faith. Note also the phrase, "the effective prayer of a righteous man." Not all prayer is effective, and not all men are righteous. Let us not assume that our own faith or right-eousness is somehow a guarantee for effective prayer. At the same time, let us consider that if we are lacking in faith and living in compromise, we cannot expect our prayer to be particularly effective.

In a strangely related passage, husbands are instructed to "live with your wives in an understanding way, as with some-one weaker, since she is a woman; and show her honor as a fellow heir of the grace of life, so that your prayers will not be hindered." **(1 Peter 3:7)** The implication is that somehow our prayers can, in fact, be hindered depending upon how we relate to our wives. We have seen that when spouses in troubled marriages commit to pray for each other, together, every day for one month, things change, and their marriages improve greatly. What may have ended in divorce is redeemed through prayer.

Finally, prayer is deeper than our understanding. Jesus taught us the basics of prayer, but thankfully, He did not leave us alone in it. "In the same way the Spirit also helps our weakness; for we do not know how to pray as we should, but the Spirit Himself intercedes for us with groanings too deep for words; and He who searches the hearts knows what the mind of the Spirit is, because He intercedes for the saints according to the will of God." **(Romans 8:26-27)** Thank God for that!

When we have some understanding of how to pray, we can better understand what to pray. This list is far from complete, but it does help us to be a bit more intentional about what to pray for and why. Among other things, we should consistently pray for:

1. **God's sovereign agenda.** "Your kingdom come; Your will be done." **(Matthew 6:10)** This life is about His kingdom, not ours. God should not only be seated upon His throne in heaven, He should also be seated on the throne of our lives here "on earth as it is in heaven." "Do not worry then, saying, 'What will we eat?' or 'What will we drink?' or 'What will we wear for clothing?' For the Gentiles eagerly seek all these things; for your heavenly Father knows that you need all these things. But seek first His kingdom and His righteousness, and all these things will be added to you." **(Matthew 6:31-33)**

2. **God's Provision.** "Give us this day our daily bread." **(Matthew 6:11)** This prayer is for sustenance, not for surplus. "For we have brought nothing into the world, so we cannot take anything out of it either. If we have food and covering, with these we shall be content." **(1 Timothy 6:7-8)** In the words of the proverb, "Give me neither poverty nor riches; feed me with the food that

is my portion, that I not be full and deny You and say, 'Who is the LORD?' or that I not be in want and steal, and profane the name of my God." **(Proverbs 30:8-9)**

3. **Forgiveness.** "Forgive us our debts." **(Matthew 6:12)** "If we say that we have no sin, we are deceiving ourselves and the truth is not in us. If we confess our sins, He is faithful and righteous to forgive us our sins and to cleanse us from all unrighteousness." **(1 John 1:8-9)** Often overlooked is the condition that we be forgiven "as we also have forgiven our debtors." "For if you forgive others for their transgressions, your heavenly Father will also forgive you. But if you do not forgive others, then your Father will not forgive your transgressions." **(Matthew 6:14-15)**

4. **Freedom from Sin.** "Lead us not into temptation, but deliver us from evil." **(Matthew 6:13)** "Let no one say when he is tempted, 'I am being tempted by God'; for God cannot be tempted by evil, and He Himself does not tempt anyone. But each one is tempted when he is carried away and enticed by his own lust." **(James 1:13-14)** "No temptation has overtaken you but such as is common to man; and God is faithful, who will not allow you to be tempted beyond what you are able, but with the temptation will provide the way of escape also, so that you will be able to endure it." **(1 Corinthians 10:13)**

5. **Wisdom.** "The fear of the Lord is the beginning of wisdom." **(Psalm 111:10)** "But if any of you lacks wisdom, let him ask of God, who gives to all generously and without reproach, and it will be given to him." **(James 1:5)**

6. **Healing.** "Is anyone among you suffering? Then he must pray. Is anyone cheerful? He is to sing praises. Is anyone among you sick? Then he must call for the elders of the church and they are to pray over him, anointing him with oil in the name of the Lord; and the prayer offered in faith will restore the one who is sick, and the Lord will raise him up, and if he has committed sins, they will be forgiven him. Therefore, confess your sins to one another, and pray for one another so that you may be healed." **(James 5:13-18)**

7. **Our Leaders.** "First of all, then, I urge that entreaties and prayers, petitions and thanksgivings, be made on behalf of all men, for kings and all who are in authority, so that we may lead a tranquil and quiet life in all godliness and dignity." **(1 Timothy 2:1-2)** Criticism comes naturally and leaders are easy targets. As Christians, we should be setting the example for less commentary and more prayer.

8. **Laborers.** "(Jesus) was saying to (His disciples), 'The harvest is plentiful, but the laborers are few; therefore beseech the Lord of the harvest to send out laborers

into His harvest.'"**(Luke 10:2)** This prayer is not for the harvest itself. The harvest is plentiful. This prayer is for laborers. God is seeking those who will join Him in the work that He has already accomplished. "Behold, I say to you, lift up your eyes and look on the fields, that they are white for harvest. Already he who reaps is receiving wages and is gathering fruit for life eternal; so that he who sows and he who reaps may rejoice together. For in this case the saying is true, 'One sows and another reaps.' I sent you to reap that for which you have not labored; others have labored and you have entered into their labor." **(John 4:35-38)**

We end this chapter with some thoughts concerning con-gregational prayer since there are some differences between praying alone and praying together. First, we should make it a habit to begin and end our meetings with prayer because it settles our hearts before God and sets the overall tone of the Church.

We should allow adequate time in our meetings to thoughtfully hear prayer requests without dragging them out too long. This requires setting clear parameters upfront in order to prevent one or two people from monopolizing the time and frustrating the group with long-winded, detailed sto-ries. We are all prone to ramble on occasion, but unless we are careful, those occasions can multiply to the point that they become the rule rather than the exception.

We should encourage each other to pray for what truly matters to us personally rather than hide behind imper-sonal prayer requests. Our regular Church gathering is not the time to pray for "a friend's cousin who needs surgery," or for "the family in the newspaper whose house just burned down," etc. Those concerns are all legitimate, but they should be prayed for separately. This is a time for us to pray together for "one another." Guidance in this area falls on leaders to lead by example and with some degree of boldness. When presented with an impersonal prayer, we respond by asking, "How does that affect you personally?" or, "How can we pray for you personally in that situation?" After a while, most of us catch on, and our prayer as a group becomes more personal and genuine.

We must absolutely refuse to allow gossip and unnecessary information about others to creep in under the guise of prayer. There is no tolerance for any of us to say, "I just had to tell you this-or-that about him-or-her so we 'can pray for them.'" If "he-or-she" is not part of our immediate group, then we are flirting with gossip. If we are committed to keeping our prayer personal, then we are much less likely to fall into this sin.

Finally, we should strive for unity in our prayer together. Big things happen when our hearts are united before God. Jesus said, "I say to you, that if two of you agree on earth about anything that they may ask, it shall be done for them by My Father who is in heaven. For where two or three have gathered together in My name, I am there in their midst." **(Matthew 18:19-20)**

CHAPTER 10

EVANGELISM

Evangelism ("euaggélion") comes from the Greek word for "gospel" (good news). Evangelism literally means, "bringing the good news". The term "evangelical" simply refers to an individual or to a church that places an emphasis on sharing the gospel with others. In reality, all who believe in Christ are called to participate in evangelism in some way, shape, or form, knowing that "whoever will call on the name of the Lord will be saved." **(Romans 10:13)** But "how then will they call on Him in whom they have not believed? How will they believe in Him whom they have not heard? And how will they hear without a preacher? How will they preach unless they are sent? Just as it is written, 'how beautiful are the feet of those who bring good news of good things!'" **(Romans 10:14-15)** The task has been given to us to "be (His) witnesses both in Jerusalem, and in all Judea and Samaria, and even to the remotest part of the earth." **(Acts 1:8)**

As Christians, our vocation can be anything, but our occupation is to "be about our Father's business." **(Luke 2:49)** If we are housekeepers, be God's housekeepers. If we are doctors, be God's doctors. Regardless of what we do for a living, we want people to hear the good news. We want them to know Jesus. Although most of us are not evangelists by profession, we all play a vital role in the process of reaching the lost. Some of us may plant, some of us may water; some of us may spend our entire lives plowing up the ground so that others may plant and water. In any case, "neither the one who plants nor the one who waters is anything, but God who causes the growth. Now he who plants and he who waters are one; but each will receive his own reward according to his own labor." **(1 Corinthians 3:7-8)**

Evangelism is a lifestyle committed to being, at all times and in all ways, an ambassador for Christ. We are called to be witnesses, testifying to our personal relationship with Jesus through our character, through our words, and through our actions. A witness is something we are before it becomes something we do. We don't "go witnessing," we <u>are</u> witnesses. Our testimony is a 24-hour-a-day, 7-day-a-week testimony. Actions do speak louder than words and our life is what will ultimately prove the validity of our testimony. "You are the light of the world. A city set on a hill cannot be hidden; nor does anyone light a lamp and put it under a basket, but on the lampstand, and it gives light to all who are in the house. Let your light shine before men in such a way that they may see your good works, and glorify your Father who is in heaven." **(Matthew 5:14-16)** Francis of Assisi (1181-1226 AD) said it well: "Preach the gospel at all times; if necessary, use words."

We have been entrusted with the most important, life-changing message that anyone will ever hear. Paul wrote, "woe is me if I do not preach the gospel." **(1 Corinthians 9:16)** "(We) are not ashamed of the gospel, for it is the power of God for salvation to everyone who believes." **(Romans 1:16)** Our commission is to "sanctify Christ as Lord in (our) hearts, always being ready to make a defense to everyone who asks (us) to give an account for the hope that is in (us), yet with gentleness and reverence." **(1 Peter 3:15)** The gospel will always be offensive, but it does not have to be obnoxious. The offense comes from the very nature of the Name. "Jesus" (Joshua; Jehovah-shua) means, "God our salvation." The implication is that we need to be saved from something (our sin). That alone is an affront to our pride and self-reliance. However, there is "no other name under heaven that has been given among men by which we must be saved." **(Acts 4:12)** Some may be offended, but our job is simply to speak the truth in love **(Ephesians 4:15)**. If our motivation is right, the message will be as well.

We often make the gospel more complicated than it really is. The simple truth is "that if (we) confess with (our) mouth Jesus as Lord, and believe in (our) heart that God raised Him from the dead, (we) will be saved." **(Romans 10:9)** There are no other strings attached. To clarify, Paul wrote, "now I make known to you, brethren, the gospel which I preached to you, which also you received, in which also you stand, by which also you are saved, if you hold fast the word which I preached to you, unless you believed in vain. For I delivered to you as of first importance what I also received, that Christ died for our sins according to the Scriptures, and that He was buried, and that He was raised on the third day according to the Scriptures..." **(1 Corinthians 5:1-5)** The power of the gospel is not the crucifixion; that Jesus died for our sin. The power of the gospel is the resurrection; that Jesus died for our sin and rose again. He conquered sin and death, and because He lives, so can we. **(Romans 6:8-10)**

Jesus' last recorded words before His ascension were for us to "go therefore and make disciples of all the nations, baptizing them in the name of the Father and the Son and the Holy Spirit, teaching them to observe all that (He) commanded (us)." **(Matthew 28:19-20)** Those final remarks are referred to as "The Great Commission" (an extra-Biblical subject heading found in most English Bibles). Jesus did not commission us to go and make converts. He commissioned us to go and make disciples. There is a big difference between the two. Just like physical fitness, spiritual fitness requires disciplined training and exercise. Many come to Christ in the short run, but few walk with Him over the long haul. Obedience is the key, and in many cases, the difference comes down to the example set by our spiritual mentors. "We desire that each one of you show the same diligence so as to realize the full assurance of hope until the end, so that you will not be sluggish, but imitators of those who through faith and patience inherit the promises." **(Hebrews 6:11-12)** Have we chosen our mentors well? Have we ourselves become good mentors to others? Can we, like Paul, say with confidence, "Be imitators of me, just as I also am of Christ?" **(1 Corinthians 11:1)**

As we have said, there are no "professional" Christians. All of us are called to the task. God has placed each one of us in a unique position to reach a unique circle of people that no one else can reach. "(We) are a chosen race, a royal priesthood, a holy nation, a people for God's own possession, so that (we) may proclaim the excellencies of Him who has called (us) out of darkness into His marvelous light; for (we) once were not a people, but now (we) are the people of God; (we) had not received mercy, but now (we) have received mercy." **(1 Peter 2:9-10)** We may not see ourselves as chosen, priestly, or holy, but that is exactly what we are according to God's Word and by His grace. Though all of us are called to evangelize, some have been especially gifted for it. "He gave some as apostles, and some as prophets, and some as evangelists, and some as pastors and teachers, for the equipping of the saints for the work of service, to the building up of the body of Christ…" **(Ephesians 4:11-12)** Perhaps you are one of these people. If so, remember that the purpose of all gifts is "for the equipping of the saints for the work of service, to the building up of the body of Christ." Those of us with roles in the spotlight must make all the more certain that the only kingdom we are building is His. We make disciples for Christ, not for ourselves.

Some will ask, "If God already knows who will be saved and who will not, then why evangelize at all?" The first reason is simple obedience to Jesus' command. **(Matthew 28:18-20)** The second is to align our hearts with the heart of God. God loves people and He wants to see the lost found. "'Do I have any pleasure in the death of the wicked,' declares the Lord God, 'rather than that he should turn from his ways and live?'" **(Ezekiel 18:23)** "The Lord is not slow about His promise, as some count slowness, but is patient toward you, not wishing for any to perish but for all to come to repentance." **(2 Peter 3:9)** "For the Son of Man has come to save that which was lost. What do you think? If any man has a hundred sheep, and one of them has gone astray, does he not leave the ninety-nine on the mountains and go and search for the one that is straying? If it turns out that he finds it, truly I say to you, he rejoices over it more than over the ninety-nine which have not gone astray. So it is not the will of your Father who is in heaven that one of these little ones perish." **(Matthew 18:11-14)** It should humble us to consider that we ourselves were once the lost. "But God demonstrates His own love toward us, in that while we were yet sinners, Christ died for us." **(Romans 5:8)** Should we not have the same love for those who have not yet believed?

The gospel is a message for everyone, everywhere. No one is excluded from the Good News. It is "an eternal gospel to preach to those who live on the earth, and to every nation and tribe and tongue and people." (**Revelation 14:6)** We've all heard the question, "What about the guy on the island who's never heard the message? How will God deal with him?" God knows how to handle such matters – that's why He's God. The more appropriate question is, "What about you and me?" We have heard the message. How will God deal with us? Nevertheless, this is why Jesus said, "You shall be My witnesses both in Jerusalem, and in all Judea and Samaria, and even to the remotest part of the earth." **(Acts 1:8)** For the first disciples, Jerusalem was their hometown in which most of their daily lives took place. In other words, Jerusalem represents our immediate family, friends, neighbors, and co-workers. Sadly, many of us never even take the time to get to know our neighbors. The most-often neglected mission field is the one in our own backyard. Before we think about reaching the lost in far away places, we should at least attempt to reach those in our circle of influence at home. True, "a prophet is not without honor except in his hometown and among his own people," **(Mark 6:4)** but we have to at least try. After Jerusalem comes Judea and Samaria. These were the surrounding towns and cities that were farther away but still considered local. The first disciples were primarily Jewish, and in that context, Judea and Samaria represented the outsiders, those who were considered unclean and excluded from the people of God. We often view others as different from ourselves, but the gospel leaves no room for prejudice of any kind. "It is not those who are well who need a physician, but those who are sick. (Jesus) did not come to call the righteous, but sinners to repentance." **(Luke 5:31-32)** All of us, regardless of our background, fall into that category. Finally, we come to the remotest parts of the earth. These represent foreign mission fields. Not everyone is called to go and serve in another country, but all of us can help through financial giving and prayer. This might mean supporting a missionary traveling overseas, or perhaps more effectively, it might mean supporting an indigenous believer reaching his own people for Christ. Either way, we should be actively involved in world missions.

The world is a big place and there are many who have never heard the gospel. Jesus told His disciples, "The harvest is plentiful, but the laborers are few; therefore beseech the Lord of the harvest to send out laborers into His harvest." **(Luke 10:2)** This prayer is not for the harvest itself. The harvest is "plentiful." This prayer is for laborers. God is looking for those who will join Him in the work that He has already accomplished. Are we up for the task? "Behold, I say to you, lift up your eyes and look on the fields, that they are white for harvest. Already he who reaps is receiving wages and is gathering fruit for life eternal; so that he who sows and he who reaps may rejoice together. For in this case the saying is true, 'One sows and another reaps.' I sent you to reap that for which you have not labored; others have labored and you have entered into their labor." **(John 4:35-38)** Jesus left no room for half-hearted pledges of commitment. "As they were going along the road, someone said to Him, 'I will follow You wherever You go.' And Jesus said to him, 'The foxes have holes and the birds of the air have nests, but the Son of Man has nowhere to lay His head.' And He said to another, 'Follow Me.' But he said, 'Lord, permit me first to go and bury my father.' But He said to him, 'Allow the dead to bury their own dead; but as for you, go and proclaim everywhere the kingdom of God.' Another also said, 'I will follow You, Lord; but first permit me to say good-bye to those at home.' But Jesus said to him, 'No one, after putting his hand to the plow and looking back, is fit for the kingdom of God.'" **(Luke 9:57-62)** Sobering words, but we are either in this fully or not at all.

Baptism

In our evangelism, we may find ourselves as the ones in the position of baptizing a new believer, so it is helpful to know a little bit about it beforehand. The Church has been given two symbolic observances in the New Testament: Communion and Baptism. Whereas communion is an ongoing commemoration of our unity as believers through Jesus' death, resurrection, and return, baptism is a one-time event, marking the beginning of our new life in Christ. For "all of us who have been baptized into Christ Jesus have been baptized into His death. Therefore we have been buried with Him through baptism into death, so that as Christ was raised from the dead through the glory of the Father, so we too might walk in newness of life." **(Romans 6:3-4)**

Baptism is best described as an outward sign of an inward change that has already taken place. Baptism does not save us, but it does serve to testify that we have been saved. Jesus Himself was baptized, setting the example for us to follow **(Matthew 3:13-15)**. We are to be baptized **(Acts 2:37-38)** and we are to baptize others when they come to faith **(Matthew 28:19-20)**. Any believer can be baptized, and any believer can baptize another. Again, there are no "professional" Christians ordained above others to perform this rite. In fact, the most meaningful baptisms are those performed by whoever has been most influential in the new believer's coming to faith (perhaps a grandmother or a close friend, etc.).

Baptism is a simple celebration that should be held as soon as possible whenever someone comes to Christ in our midst. There is no need for a waiting period. We remember the eunuch who said to Phillip, "Look! Water! What prevents me from being baptized?" **(Acts 8:36)**. He didn't delay or go through a class; he just went and got baptized right away. There is nothing special about the water. We can use whatever is available (a river, a bathtub, a garden hose, etc.). There is nothing special about the place. We can baptize anywhere (in a church building, in a home, in a park, etc.). Though there are several methods of baptism ranging from sprinkling to submersion, no particular method is mandated in the Bible. We prefer submersion because it more visually symbolizes the spiritual death, burial, and resurrection of the believer in Christ. As for what to say, we try to keep it simple and personal. The following (pieced together from **2 Corinthians 5:17, Romans 6:4,** and **Matthew 28:19**) is an example for those who might be at a loss for words when baptizing:

"If anyone is in Christ, he is a new creature. The old things have passed away and new things have come. We are buried with Christ through baptism, so that as Christ was raised from the dead, we too might walk in newness of life (Pause here and encourage the new believer to say a few words to the witnesses if he/she wants to do so). *It is my honor and privilege to baptize you* (insert name), *my brother/sister, in the name of the Father, and the Son, and the Holy Spirit…* (Baptize him/her)"

Seeing people come to faith in Christ and being baptized is one of the most uplifting events that we have the privilege of witnessing. They have gone from death to life, and it just doesn't get any better than that. "I tell you, there is joy in the presence of the angels of God over one sinner who repents." **(Luke 15:10)**

C H A P T E R   1 1

THE CHURCH

The word, "church" (ekklesia) literally means, "called out," and is defined as "a group of free citizens called together into an assembly." There are countless local churches, but there is only one Church. "There is one body and one Spirit, just as also you were called in one hope of your calling; one Lord, one faith, one baptism, one God and Father of all who is over all and through all and in all." **(Ephesians 4:4-6)** Through our common faith, we the Church are "the household of God…the pillar and support of the truth." **(1 Timothy 3:15)**

The early believers understood that Church refers to people, not to buildings. "Day by day continuing with one mind in the temple, and breaking bread from house to house, they were taking their meals together with gladness and sincerity of heart, praising God and having favor with all the people. And the Lord was adding to their number day by day those who were being saved…and everyday, in the temple and from house to house, they kept right on teaching and preaching Jesus as the Christ." **(Acts 2:46-47; 5:42)** Throughout the Bible, we see the Church functioning both in the home and in larger assemblies. Both forms are necessary, but we have to be clear about the nature and purpose of each and how they work together. On the one hand, when we gather together in larger groups ("in the temple"), it is for a public time of celebration, instruction, and exhortation (a message to unbelievers). On the other hand, when we gather together in our homes ("from house to house"), it is for a more private, intimate time of discipleship, fellowship, communion, and prayer that simply cannot be achieved in a larger assembly. Throughout the New Testament, we more often read, "Greet the church that is in their house." **(Romans 16:5, 1 Corinthians 16:19, Colossians 4:15, Philemon 1:2)** Perhaps the best perspective is to view the larger gathering as an assembly of related house churches that come together frequently for a shared time of celebration, instruction, and exhortation. On a side note, the temple and Solomon's portico were both public places that could accommodate large crowds and where anyone could meet for free. It wasn't until after Christianity was recognized by the Roman government (about 300-400 years after the birth of the Church) that buildings were specifically constructed for Christian gatherings. Before then, the Church met in private homes and, throughout much of the world, it still does today.

Over the centuries, we have accumulated volumes of man-made traditions and misconceptions that must be overcome before we can begin to experience genuine, Biblical Church. For example, consider our initial reaction to the following questions: Where do you go to church on Sunday? Are you a member? What does church look like? Although the Bible does refer to the day after the Sabbath (Saturday) as "the first day of the week" **(Matthew 28:1)**, and we do see examples of Christians gathering on Sundays **(John 20:19, Acts 20:7)**, there is no Biblical mandate as to the day of the week on which we must meet. What we do know for sure is that "the Sabbath was made for man, and not man for the Sabbath," **(Mark 2:27)** that "where two or three have gathered together in (Jesus') Name, (He is) there in (our) midst," **(Matthew 18:20)** and that we should "not forsake (our) assembling together." **(Hebrews 10:25)** We are not given much beyond that. If one group of believers meets in a private home on a Tuesday evening, and another group of believers meets in a public building on a Sunday morning, we must acknowledge that both are, in fact, the Church. As for membership, most churches have formalities in place due to the fact that corporate law deems it necessary for a legally recognized organization to distinguish between voting and non-voting "members" (one of the many burdens associated with a corpus (body) of individuals owning buildings and other shared assets together). However, there is no scriptural or spiritual basis for that definition of member-ship within the Church. We are either personally committed to our local church body or we are not. These are just a few of the many obstacles that get in the way of our experiencing genuine, Biblical Church. In our fellowship together, we should constantly evaluate whether our practice is based on the Bible or on our own rituals. Our freedom in fellowship was paid for by the blood of Christ, so let us be careful not to "invalidate the word of God for the sake of (our) traditions." **(Matthew 15:6)**

As much as we have freedom in our fellowship, we also have order. Christ alone is the head of the Church. He alone is our perfect example. "He is also head of the body, the church; and He is the beginning, the firstborn from the dead, so that He Himself will come to have first place in everything." **(Colossians 1:18)** As the Church grew larger, the need arose for some type of leadership structure that would accommodate more people. The Bible has much to say regarding our responsibilities and God's expectations when it comes to man's leadership within the Church. These clearly defined requirements and qualifications have nothing to do with academic credentials or professional status. "For consider your calling, brethren, that there were not many wise according to the flesh, not many mighty, not many noble; but God has chosen the foolish things of the world to shame the wise, and God has chosen the weak things of the world to shame the things which are strong, and the base things of the world and the despised God has chosen, the things that are not, so that He may nullify the things that are, so that no man may boast before God." **(1 Corinthians 1:26-29)** Jesus Himself had no earthly credentials to speak of. He did not go to seminary. He did not go to rabbinical school. He had no ordination papers. He was the son of a carpenter, yet He was the Messiah all the same. His words and deeds attest to the fact. Even so, "He came to His hometown and began teaching them in their synagogue, so that they were astonished, and said, 'Where did this man get this wisdom and these miraculous powers? Is not this the carpenter's son? Is not His mother called Mary, and His brothers, James and Joseph and Simon and Judas? And His sisters, are they not all with us? Where then did this man get all these things?' And they took offense at Him. But Jesus said to them, 'A prophet is not without honor except in his hometown and in his own household.' And He did not do many miracles there because of their unbelief." **(Matthew 13:54-58)** We must be careful that in our due diligence to qualify and to preserve righteous order within the Church, we don't overlook those who are truly called by God to minister within the body of Christ. At the same time, we must not dilute the leadership of the Church by allowing those who are not called or qualified (regardless of education or credentials) to enter the ministry. It is a difficult balance requiring a great deal of discernment.

Leadership is service. Whether or not we are called to lead, we are all called to serve the body of Christ with the gifts that He has given us. "Now there are varieties of gifts, but the same Spirit. And there are varieties of ministries, and the same Lord. There are varieties of effects, but the same God who works all things in all persons. But to each one is given the manifestation of the Spirit for the common good." **(1 Corinthians 12:4-7)** "Since we have gifts that differ according to the grace given to us, each of us is to exercise them accordingly: if prophecy, according to the proportion of his faith; if service, in his serving; or he who teaches, in his teaching; or he who exhorts, in his exhortation; he who gives, with liberality; he who leads, with diligence; he who shows mercy, with cheerfulness." **(Romans 12:6-8)** "As each one has received a special gift, employ it in serving one another as good stewards of the manifold grace of God. Whoever speaks, is to do so as one who is speaking the utterances of God; whoever serves is to do so as one who is serving by the strength which God supplies; so that in all things God may be glorified through Jesus Christ, to whom belongs the glory and dominion forever and ever. Amen." **(1 Peter 4:10-11)**

Leadership is humble. Jesus tells us, "Do not be called Rabbi; for One is your Teacher, and you are all brothers. Do not call anyone on earth your father; for One is your Father, He who is in heaven. Do not be called leaders; for One is your Leader, that is, Christ. But the greatest among you shall be your servant." **(Matthew 23:8-11)** This does not mean that we have to fear using the words leader or teacher to make reference to these people. We clearly see them referred to this way throughout the New Testament (**1 Corinthians 12:28, Ephesians 4:11, Hebrews 5:12, 13:17, 24**) and we have to call them something for the sake of clarity. The idea is not to allow the title to become a badge of arrogance and control. "You know that those who are recognized as rulers of the Gentiles lord it over them; and their great men exercise authority over them. But it is not this way among you, but whoever wishes to become great among you shall be your servant; and whoever wishes to be first among you shall be slave of all. For even the Son of Man did not come to be served, but to serve, and to give His life a ransom for many." **(Mark 10:42-45)** As the Church, we are to "obey (our) leaders and submit to them, for they keep watch over (our) souls as those who will give an account. Let them do this with joy and not with grief, for this would be unprofitable for (us)." **(Hebrews 13:17)** Most importantly, and especially considering the great responsibility involved, we are to pray diligently for our leaders. **(1 Timothy 2:1-2, Hebrews 13:18)**

Leadership is a calling. Whether in a small house church or in a larger congregation, if we are called, we should lead. If we are not called, we should not lead. If we think we might be called, but are unsure, we have clear, Biblical instruction to guide us through the process. **1 & 2 Timothy and Titus** are often referred to as the pastoral epistles because they address many personal and administrative issues within the Church. These books give us a clear picture of the character and qualities of leaders within the body of Christ and they provide guidelines for the roles and qualifications specific to these leaders.

Though all of us are able ministers of the gospel **(2 Corinthians 3:5-6)**, the Bible refers to "elders" and "deacons" as the ones especially entrusted with tending to the people of God placed within their care. The separation of these two roles can be seen in **Acts 6** and it came about for very practical reasons. "Now at this time while the disciples were increasing in number, a complaint arose on the part of the Hellenistic Jews against the native Hebrews, because their widows were being overlooked in the daily serving of food. So the twelve summoned the congregation of the disciples and said, 'It is not desirable for us to neglect the word of God in order to serve tables. Therefore, brethren, select from among you seven men of good reputation, full of the Spirit and of wisdom, whom we may put in charge of this task. But we will devote ourselves to prayer and to the ministry of the word.' The statement found approval with the whole congregation; and they chose Stephen, a man full of faith and of the Holy Spirit, and Philip, Prochorus, Nicanor, Timon, Parmenas and Nicolas, a proselyte from Antioch. And these they brought before the apostles; and after praying, they laid their hands on them." **(Acts 6:1-6)** As everyone worked together, the result was that "the word of God kept on spreading; and the number of the disciples continued to increase greatly in Jerusalem, and a great many of the priests were becoming obedient to the faith." **(Acts 6:7)** So here we see the two roles working hand in hand. But what exactly are elders and deacons?

"Elder" (presbúteros – an old man; an ambassador) is interchangeable with "overseer/bishop" (epískopos – a watchman) and "pastor" (poimen - shepherd). A group of elders (presbutérion) is often called the "presbytery" or "council of elders." The elders are called to "shepherd the flock of God." **(1 Peter 5:2)** They are to "be on guard for (themselves) and for all the flock, among which the Holy Spirit has made (them) overseers, to shepherd the church of God which He purchased with His own blood." **(Acts 20:28)** Elders are involved in teaching and government within the Church, with their primary attention being given "to prayer and to the ministry of the word." **(Acts 6:4)** In short, they are pastor-teachers, with Christ being the ultimate "Shepherd and Guardian (epískopos)" of us all. **(1 Peter 2:25)** "Elder" is the title, referring to the dignity of the office, while "overseer," "bishop," and "pastor" are job descriptions, referring to the duties and to the authority of the office. The terms "elder" and "pastor" refer to the same person(s). We do not find terms such as "lay pastor" or "facilitator" in the Bible. One is either an elder/pastor or he is not. It's that simple. If we ever hope to establish a healthy Church, we must get past the distinction between staff (paid/vocational) and lay (unpaid/non-vocational) elders. We must publicly acknowledge the genuine, Biblical truth that an unpaid pastor of a small group meeting in the home is every bit as much a pastor as one who is paid to lead a larger congregation meeting in a church building. This conviction must start with those of us who currently serve as pastors/elders before we can expect it to spread to our congregations.

As shepherds, elders are entrusted with the spiritual care of God's people. "Jesus said to Simon Peter, "Simon, son of John, do you love Me more than these?" He said to Him, "Yes, Lord; You know that I love You." He said to him, "Tend My lambs." He said to him again a second time, "Simon, son of John, do you love Me?" He said to Him, "Yes, Lord; You know that I love You." He said to him, Shepherd My sheep." He said to him the third time, "Simon, son of John, do you love Me?" Peter was grieved because He said to him the third time, "Do you love Me?" And he said to Him, "Lord, You know all things; You know that I love You." Jesus said to him, "Tend My sheep." **(John 21:15-17)** Good shepherds tend the sheep by guiding them into good grazing land and raising them to be able to feed themselves. Likewise, good elders provide spiritual care by guiding the Church into consistent Bible study, fellowship, communion, and prayer, and by fostering an atmosphere in which other members are encouraged to use their own spiritual gifts. In the process of caring so much for others, there can be a natural tendency for elders to try to manage areas that are outside of the realm of eldership. Elders need to be aware of this tendency and make a conscious effort to allow others to carry out their God-given ministry. This requires a commitment to delegate responsibilities, then to let go of those responsibilities once delegated. "The things which you have heard me say in the presence of many witnesses, entrust these to faithful men who will be able to teach others also." **(2 Timothy 2:2)**

A "deacon" (diákonos – servant) is a hands-on minister within the Church. Deacons serve in the various tasks that must be done in order to allow for effective prayer and for the ministry of the Word to flow freely. Their help is practical and is especially geared toward the basic necessities of life. "If a brother or sister is without clothing and in need of daily food, and one of you says to them, 'Go in peace, be warmed and be filled,' and yet you do not give them what is necessary for their body, what use is that?" **(James 2:15-1)** There are many needs to be met within the Church, and by meeting those needs in practical ways we truly show the love of God. "We know love by this, that He laid down His life for us; and we ought to lay down our lives for the brethren. But whoever has the world's goods, and sees his brother in need and closes his heart against him, how does the love of God abide in him? Little children, let us not love with word or with tongue, but in deed and truth." **(1 John 3:16-18)** Jesus gave us a clear picture of deacon ministry in the following parable: "Then the King will say to those on His right, 'Come, you who are blessed of My Father, inherit the kingdom prepared for you from the foundation of the world. 'For I was hungry, and you gave Me something to eat; I was thirsty, and you gave Me something to drink; I was a stranger, and you invited Me in; naked, and you clothed Me; I was sick, and you visited Me; I was in prison, and you came to Me.' "Then the righteous will answer Him, 'Lord, when did we see You hungry, and feed You, or thirsty, and give You something to drink? 'And when did we see You a stranger, and invite You in, or naked, and clothe You? 'When did we see You sick, or in prison, and come to You?' "The King will answer and say to them, 'Truly I say to you, to the extent that you did it to one of these brothers of Mine, even the least of them, you did it to Me.'" **(Matthew 25:34-40)**

With the exception of leading in teaching and prayer, most of the day-to-day operations are handled by the deacons. Children's ministries, relaying information, coordinating events, planning outreaches, etc. all fall into the deacon category. If the congregation does have a building, the deacons should be the ones who handle its administration and maintenance. Since they do manage so much, there can be a natural tendency for deacons to try to manage areas that fall into the realm of eldership. Deacons need to be aware of this tendency, and must make a conscious effort to allow the elders to guide the spiritual direction of the church. To lead in any capacity within a local congregation, one should be willing to submit to the authority of the elders of that congregation. When all is in proper working order, each of us serving diligently in our respective roles, the partnership between elders and deacons is a harmonious one that strengthens the Church and brings joy to the body of Christ.

The roles of elder and deacon are so necessary and so interwoven that there is no removing of one without the dissolving of the other. There is no weakening of one without the breaking down of the other. "And if one member suffers, all the members suffer with it; if one member is honored, all the members rejoice with it." **(1 Corinthians 12:26)** Likewise, we are only effective when we are serving within the capacity of our own calling. Not all of us were made to be elders nor were all of us made to be deacons. "Now you are Christ's body, and individually members of it. And God has appointed in the church, first apostles, second prophets, third teachers, then miracles, then gifts of healings, helps, administrations, various kinds of tongues. All are not apostles, are they? All are not prophets, are they? All are not teachers, are they? All are not workers of miracles, are they? All do not have gifts of healings, do they? All do not speak with tongues, do they? All do not interpret, do they?" **(1 Corinthians 12:27-30)** "But to each one of us grace was given according to the measure of Christ's gift." **(Ephesians 4:4-7)** "And He gave some as apostles, and some as prophets, and some as evangelists, and some as pastors and teachers, for the equipping of the saints for the work of service, to the building up of the body of Christ; until we all attain to the unity of the faith, and of the knowledge of the Son of God, to a mature man, to the measure of the stature which belongs to the fullness of Christ. As a result, we are no longer to be children, tossed here and there by waves and carried about by every wind of doctrine, by the trickery of men, by craftiness in deceitful scheming; but speaking the truth in love, we are to grow up in all aspects into Him who is the head, even Christ, from whom the whole body, being fitted and held together by what every joint supplies, according to the proper working of each individual part, causes the growth of the body for the building up of itself in love." **(Ephesians 4:11-16)**

We should each have a clear understanding of who God has made us to be. We should then serve in that capacity with our whole heart to build up the body of Christ. We should also understand the boundaries of our particular role and the boundaries of the roles of others within the body in order to work together in unity. Tools are most effective when they are used for their intended purpose. An elder doing the work of a deacon or a deacon doing the work of an elder is like using a wrench as a hammer or a hammer as a wrench. The results are bad and the tools get broken. That being said, let us take a closer look at what makes each role uniquely suited for its specific purpose…

Qualifications of an Elder

We are given the most details about the qualifications of an elder. As we go through the list, we begin to understand why Paul wrote, "The elders who rule well are to be considered worthy of double honor, especially those who work hard at preaching and teaching." **(1 Timothy 5:17)** We hold these men in high regard because there are simply not many of them to be found. "It is a trustworthy statement: if any man aspires to the office of overseer, it is a fine work he desires to do. An overseer, then, must be…"**(1 Timothy 3:1-7, Titus 1:6-9)**

1. **Above reproach** (anepíleptos). Literally, 'unable to be seized.' Another word is 'anégkletos,' meaning, 'not accused; free from any legal charge.' The idea is that there is nothing in an elder's life that the enemy can take hold of (seize) to discredit the faith. Accusations may still come, but those accusations have no solid ground on which to stand. One of the best examples is found in the person of Daniel: "It seemed good to Darius to appoint 120 satraps over the kingdom, that

they would be in charge of the whole kingdom, and over them three commissioners (of whom Daniel was one), that these satraps might be accountable to them, and that the king might not suffer loss. Then this Daniel began distinguishing himself among the commissioners and satraps because he possessed an extraordinary spirit, and the king planned to appoint him over the entire kingdom. Then the commissioners and satraps began trying to find a ground of accusation against Daniel in regard to government affairs; but they could find no ground of accusation or evidence of corruption, inasmuch as he was faithful, and no negligence or corruption was to be found in him. Then these men said, 'We will not find any ground of accusation against this Daniel unless we find it against him with regard to the law of his God.'" **(Daniel 6:1-5)** Peter puts it this way, "Keep your behavior excellent among the Gentiles, so that in the thing in which they slander you as evildoers, they may because of your good deeds, as they observe them, glorify God in the day of visitation." **(1 Peter 2:12)**

2. **The husband of one wife.** This clearly refers to having only one wife at a time; no polygamy; we all agree on that. We also agree that one may remarry if his previous wife has died. We even agree (for the most part) that one may be divorced and still be an elder, provided the divorce was on the grounds of marital unfaithfulness **(Matthew 5:31-32; 19:9)**. The real debate comes with the issue of remarriage after divorce, a situation that

Scripture clearly equates with adultery **(Mark 10:11-12, Luke 16:18)**. Though many have tried, we cannot limit this requirement simply to the banning of polygamy. The wording is difficult, but **1 Timothy 5:9** sheds light on the subject. This passage refers to widows, and it uses nearly identical language. It says, "A widow is to be put on the list only if she is not less than 60 years old, the wife of one man..." Polygamy can be of two types: "polygyny" (one man married to many women) and "polyandry" (one woman married to many men). In Biblical cultures, polygyny (one man, many women) was sometimes seen, whereas polyandry (one woman, many men) was completely prohibited. In light of this fact, **1 Timothy 5:9** more clearly reads, "having been the wife of one man," since the woman of this passage most certainly would not have been married to more than one husband at a time.

As divorce becomes more and more prevalent within the Church, the tendency is to accept or to avoid the situation (so-and-so is a good, upstanding man, a solid believer, and no one else will step up. Yes, he's divorced and remarried, but...). However, an honest look at Scripture shows us quite clearly that this requirement does, in fact, disqualify from eldership (but not from service or fellowship) those who have remarried after divorce. It upholds the first requirement of not having anything that the enemy can take hold of to discredit the faith. What we must understand is that a higher calling is being presented here; something much bigger than whether or not it is OK for a believer to remarry after divorce. Eldership is a calling that gives all for the sake of Christ and for His Church. There are no compromises. Paul says, "I think then that this is good in view of the present distress, that it is good for a man to remain as he is. Are you bound to a wife? Do not seek to be released. Are you released from a wife? Do not seek a wife. But if you marry, you have not sinned; and if a virgin marries, she has not sinned. Yet such will have trouble in this life, and I am trying to spare you." **(1 Corinthians 7:26-28)** This may be a difficult truth for some to swallow, but if we ever expect to be the Church that truly honors God, then we need to play by His rules, not by ours. The issue frequently comes up where a person with a history of divorce and remarriage wants to lead as an elder. Strong emotions are almost always involved, so we must be sensitive as we hold to the standard of God's Word. When confronted with such a scenario, we like to point to **1 Chronicles 22**. This passage tells the story of King David wanting to build the Temple. However, God would not allow him to build it because he was a 'man of war.' It would be David's son, Solomon, who would go on to build the Temple. David could have been bitter, but instead, his response was to acknowledge God's Word by joyfully helping Solomon prepare for building the Temple. David may not have built the building, but it would not have been possible without him. Again, a man may be disqualified from eldership, but not from fellowship or service in other capacities.

3. **Temperate** (nephálios). Sober; sober-minded; self-controlled. A state of mind that is free from the excessive influence of passion, lust, or emotion. A consistent personality brings stability to the spectrum of emotional issues that arise within the Church.

4. **Prudent** (sophron). Understanding; wise; sensible. To understand is to be so thoroughly familiar with something that we clearly know its character, nature, and subtleties. This kind of understanding only comes from personal experience. Such experience is only gained over time, lending more credibility to the term 'elder.'

5. **Respectable** (kósmios). Orderly; not "self-willed" (authádes). Quietly fulfilling our duties, while voluntarily placing limitations on our own freedom for the sake of Christ and others. This is about making the most of our limited time and energy. As Paul wrote, "All things are lawful, but not all things are profitable. All things are lawful, but not all things edify. Let no one seek his own good, but that of his neighbor." **(1 Corinthians 10:23-24)** "Therefore be careful how you walk, not as unwise men but as wise, making the most of your time, because the days are evil." **(Ephesians 5:15-16)**

6. **Hospitable** (philóxenos). Literally, 'a friend of strangers.' Hospitality is keeping an open door and a willingness to be inconvenienced and at times interrupted as a minister of the gospel. We are told not to "neglect to show hospitality to strangers, for by this some have entertained angels without knowing it." **(Hebrews 13:2)**

7. **Able to teach** (didaktikós). Skilled at communicating Biblical truth. Great responsibility is attached to teaching, and this is one of the major requirements listed for elders that is not listed for deacons. Not all elders teach, but all elders are to be able to teach. James says, "Let not many of you become teachers, my brethren, knowing that as such we will incur a stricter judgment." **(James 3:1)** The warning here is appropriate and given for good reason "for some men, straying from these things, have turned aside to fruitless discussion, wanting to be teachers of the Law, even though they do not understand either what they are saying or the matters about which they make confident assertions." **(1 Timothy 1:6-7)** A teacher is entrusted with "holding fast the faithful word which is in accordance with the teaching, so that he will be able both to exhort in sound doctrine and to refute those who contradict. For there are many rebellious men, empty talkers and deceivers, especially those of the circumcision, who must be silenced because they are upsetting whole families, teaching things they should not teach for the sake of sordid gain." **(Titus 1:9-11)** With teaching

comes the call to a life of diligence. Although God is the One who calls the teacher **(Ephesians 4:11)**, the calling to teach still requires the disciplined, ongoing study of God's Word. "For though by this time you ought to be teachers, you have need again for someone to teach you the elementary principles of the oracles of God, and you have come to need milk and not solid food. For everyone who partakes only of milk is not accustomed to the word of righteousness, for he is an infant. But solid food is for the mature, who because of practice have their senses trained to discern good and evil." **(Hebrews 5:12-14)** The stakes are high, and the exhortation is to, "pay close attention to yourself and to your teaching; persevere in these things, for as you do this you will ensure salvation both for yourself and for those who hear you." **(1 Timothy 4:16)**

8. **Not addicted to wine** (pároinos). Literally, 'not near wine.' This refers to the constant use of alcohol. The word picture is that of an individual who always has a bottle on the table. Paul writes, "Do not get drunk with wine, for that is dissipation (wasteful extravagance), but be filled with the Spirit." **(Ephesians 5:18)** Drunkenness is clearly prohibited whereas drinking itself is not. However, considering all of the negative associations with alcohol, its expense, and the fact that so many of our brothers and sisters have stumbled over it, we personally believe that we should prayerfully consider cutting it out completely. Paul sums up the attitude best when he says, "for if someone sees you,

who have knowledge, dining in an idol's temple, will not his conscience, if he is weak, be strengthened to eat things sacrificed to idols? For through your knowledge he who is weak is ruined, the brother for whose sake Christ died. And so, by sinning against the brethren and wounding their conscience when it is weak, you sin against Christ. Therefore, if food causes my brother to stumble, I will never eat meat again, so that I will not cause my brother to stumble." **(1 Corinthians 8:10-13)**

9. **Not pugnacious** (plektes). Not inclined to quarrel or fight; not quick-tempered (orgílos). There is a balance between submission and standing up for the truth. Some battles must be fought, but we must choose our battles wisely. We are to "refuse foolish and ignorant speculations, knowing that they produce quarrels," **(2 Timothy 2:23)** and we are to "avoid foolish controversies and genealogies and strife and disputes about the Law, for they are unprofitable and worthless." **(Titus 3:9)** Even when a battle must be fought, it must be fought rightly. "The Lord's bond-servant must not be quarrelsome, but be kind to all, able to teach, patient when wronged, with gentleness correcting those who are in opposition."**(2 Timothy 2:24-25)** We are told to, "reject a factious man after a first and second warning, knowing that such a man is perverted and is sinning, being self-condemned." **(Titus 3:10-11)** Our example is Christ Himself: "Behold, My Servant whom I have chosen; My beloved in whom My soul is well-pleased; I will put My Spirit upon Him, and he shall proclaim

justice to the Gentiles. He will not quarrel, nor cry out; nor will anyone hear His voice in the streets." **(Matthew 12:18-19)**

10. **Gentle** (epieikes). Fair; appropriate for the situation. Different circumstances and personalities require different approaches. We must be sensitive enough to "let (our) speech always be with grace, as though seasoned with salt, so that (we) will know how (we) should respond to each person." **(Colossians 4:6)**

11. **Peaceable** (ámachos). Without battle. This is the positive, proactive counterpart to #9. A practical description is found in **Romans 12:17-21**: "Never pay back evil for evil to anyone. Respect what is right in the sight of all men. If possible, so far as it depends on you, be at peace with all men. Never take your own revenge, beloved, but leave room for the wrath of God, for it is written, 'Vengeance is Mine, I will repay', says the Lord. 'But if your enemy is hungry, feed him, and if he is thirsty, give him a drink; for in so doing you will heap burning coals on his head.' Do not be overcome by evil, but overcome evil with good."

12. **Free from the love of money** (aphilárguros). This word conveys the idea of being content while trusting God to provide. "Make sure that your character is free from the love of money, being content with what you have; for He Himself has said, 'I will never desert you, nor will I ever forsake you.'" **(Hebrews 13:5-6)** Paul wrote, "I have

learned to be content in whatever circumstances I am. I know how to get along with humble means, and I also know how to live in prosperity; in any and every circumstance I have learned the secret of being filled and going hungry, both of having abundance and suffering need. I can do all things through Him who strengthens me." **(Philippians 4:11-13)** "Godliness actually is a means of great gain when accompanied by contentment. For we have brought nothing into the world, so we cannot take anything out of it either. If we have food and covering, with these we shall be content. But those who want to get rich fall into temptation and a snare and many foolish and harmful desires which plunge men into ruin and destruction. For the love of money is a root of all sorts of evil, and some by longing for it have wandered away from the faith and pierced themselves with many griefs." **(1 Timothy 6:6-10)**

13. **One who manages** (proistemi) **his own household well.** To diligently rule over and care for one's family. We are told that an elder's children are to be trustworthy (pistós), and that he is to keep them "under control with all dignity." Kids will still be kids. The real test is in our exercise of consistent, loving discipline. Poor discipline and chaos in the home are indicators that priorities are out of line and that more time and attention should be given to the family. This requirement also includes providing for the family's physical needs. "But if anyone does not provide for his own, and especially for those of his household, he has denied the faith and

is worse than an unbeliever." **(1 Timothy 5:8)** The general idea is that, "if a man does not know how to manage his own household, how will he take care of the church of God?" **(1 Timothy 3:5)**

14. **Not a new convert** (neophutos). Literally, 'not newly planted.' "So that he will not become conceited and fall into the condemnation incurred by the devil." **(1 Timothy 3:6)** Pride is so very present within all of us, but we are better able to keep it under control when we've had some time to walk with Christ. Again, we use the term 'elder' because it implies time in the Lord. For those of us charged with the responsibility of appointing elders, time allows us to make our decisions based on the evidence of good fruit in a candidate's life. As pastors, we are warned to "not lay hands upon anyone too hastily and thereby share responsibility for the sins of others." **(1 Timothy 5:22)**

15. **A good reputation** (marturía- testimony) **with those outside the church** so that he will not fall into reproach and the snare of the devil. It has been said that our lives are the only Bible that some will ever read. Our conduct should be as honorable with unbelievers as it is with believers. There is no room for hypocrisy or double standards. "For so the Lord has commanded us, 'I have placed you as a light for the Gentiles, that you may bring salvation to the end of the earth.'" **(Acts 13:47)** "Let your light shine before men in such a way

that they may see your good works, and glorify your Father who is in heaven." **(Matthew 5:16)**

16. **Loving what is good** (philágathos). Loving and practicing what is good. This combines not only the wanting to be good, but the actual doing of the good as well. We are told to, "abhor what is evil; cling to what is good" **(Romans 12:9)** and to, "set (our) minds on the things above, not on the things that are on earth." **(Colossians 3:2)** "Finally, brethren, whatever is true, whatever is honorable, whatever is right, whatever is pure, whatever is lovely, whatever is of good repute, if there is any excellence and if anything worthy of praise, dwell on these things. The things you have learned and received and heard and seen in me, practice these things, and the God of peace will be with you." **(Philippians 4:8-9)**

17. **Just** (díkaios) and **devout** (hósios). Both are similar words meaning that we are to pattern our lives by God's standards and laws, knowing that He is the only One who is truly "just and the justifier of the one who has faith in Jesus." **(Romans 3:26)** Again, this assumes our putting thoughts into action, "for it is not the hearers of the Law who are just before God, but the doers of the Law will be justified." **(Romans 2:13)**

Qualifications of a Deacon

The qualifications of deacons are similar to those of elders but with some important variations specific to the role. We are told that, "those who have served well as deacons obtain for themselves a high standing and great confidence in the faith that is in Christ Jesus." **(1 Timothy 3:13)** "Deacons likewise must be…" **(1 Timothy 3:8-12)**

1. **Men of dignity** (semnós). Venerable (commanding respect); serious. "When I was a child, I used to speak like a child, think like a child, reason like a child; when I became a man, I did away with childish things." **(1 Corinthians 13:11)**

2. **Not double-tongued** (dílogos). Not hypocritical or contradictory in speech. This has to do with integrity and consistency, walking in truth at all times regardless of outside pressure or influence. "But let your statement be, 'Yes, yes' or 'No, no'; anything beyond these is of evil." **(Matthew 5:37)**

3. **Not addicted** (prosécho) **to much wine**. See #8 for "Qualifications of an Elder." Not paying attention to, nor having the mind held toward something. This is a nautical term that signifies the holding of a ship on its course. Although the world pressures us to follow its course, the deacon holds fast to the course set by God. "And you were dead in your trespasses and sins, in which you formerly walked according to the course of this world, according to the prince of the power of the

air, of the spirit that is now working in the sons of diso-
bedience. Among them we too all formerly lived in the
lusts of our flesh, indulging the desires of the flesh and
of the mind, and were by nature children of wrath, even
as the rest. But God, being rich in mercy, because of His
great love with which He loved us, even when we were
dead in our transgressions, made us alive together
with Christ." **(Ephesians 2:1-5)**

4. **Not fond of sordid gain** (aischrokerdes). Unwilling to
   compromise integrity or moral character to gain or to
   save money. God is calling us to a higher standard and
   He will honor only that which is done His way. The ends
   do not justify the means. "For what does it profit a man
   to gain the whole world, and forfeit his soul? For what
   will a man give in exchange for his soul?" **(Mark 8:36-
   37)** "No one can serve two masters; for either he will
   hate the one and love the other, or he will be devoted
   to one and despise the other. You cannot serve God
   and wealth. For this reason I say to you, do not be worried about your life, as to what you will eat or what
   you will drink; nor for your body, as to what you will
   put on. Is not life more than food, and the body more
   than clothing? Look at the birds of the air, that they do
   not sow, nor reap nor gather into barns, and yet your
   heavenly Father feeds them. Are you not worth much
   more than they? And who of you by being worried can
   add a single hour to his life? And why are you worried about clothing? Observe how the lilies of the field
   grow; they do not toil nor do they spin, yet I say to you

that not even Solomon in all his glory clothed himself like one of these. But if God so clothes the grass of the field, which is alive today and tomorrow is thrown into the furnace, will He not much more clothe you? You of little faith! Do not worry then, saying, 'What will we eat?' or 'What will we drink?' or 'What will we wear for clothing?' For the Gentiles eagerly seek all these things; for your heavenly Father knows that you need all these things. But seek first His kingdom and His righteousness, and all these things will be added to you." **(Matthew 6:24-33)**

5. **Holding to the mystery of the faith with a clear conscience.** Here is the mystery of the faith: "And when I came to you, brethren, I did not come with superiority of speech or of wisdom, proclaiming to you the testimony of God. For I determined to know nothing among you except Jesus Christ, and Him crucified. I was with you in weakness and in fear and in much trembling, and my message and my preaching were not in persuasive words of wisdom, but in demonstration of the Spirit and of power, so that your faith would not rest on the wisdom of men, but on the power of God. Yet we do speak wisdom among those who are mature; a wisdom, however, not of this age nor of the rulers of this age, who are passing away; but we speak God's wisdom in a mystery, the hidden wisdom which God predestined before the ages to our glory; the wisdom which none of the rulers of this age has understood; for if they had understood it they would not

have crucified the Lord of glory; but just as it is written, "things which eye has not seen and ear has not heard, and which have not entered the heart of man, all that God has prepared for those who love Him." For to us God revealed them through the Spirit; for the Spirit searches all things, even the depths of God. For who among men knows the thoughts of a man except the spirit of the man which is in him? Even so the thoughts of God no one knows except the Spirit of God. Now we have received, not the spirit of the world, but the Spirit who is from God, so that we may know the things freely given to us by God, which things we also speak, not in words taught by human wisdom, but in those taught by the Spirit, combining spiritual thoughts with spiritual words. But a natural man does not accept the things of the Spirit of God, for they are foolishness to him; and he cannot understand them, because they are spiritually appraised. But he who is spiritual appraises all things, yet he himself is appraised by no one. For who has known the mind of the Lord, that he will instruct Him? But we have the mind of Christ." **(1 Corinthians 2:1-16)**

6. **These men must also first be tested** (dokimázo). Proven over time. Nothing is proven until it is actually tested in real-life circumstances. Spiritual testing of this kind comes in stages. "He who is faithful in a very little thing is faithful also in much; and he who is unrighteous in a very little thing is unrighteous also in much." **(Luke 16:10)** The elders responsible for

acknowledging and overseeing the deacons should be careful not to give too much responsibility too fast. Again, we are warned to "not lay hands upon anyone too hastily and thereby share responsibility for the sins of others." **(1 Timothy 5:22)**

7. **Beyond reproach** (anégkle tos). See #1 for "Qualifications of an Elder."

8. **Husbands of only one wife.** See #2 for "Qualifications of an Elder."

9. **Good managers of their children and their own households.** See #13 for "Qualifications of an Elder."

Qualifications of a Deaconess

Much argument is made regarding the role of women in the Church. The central texts in the debate are **1 Corinthians 14:34-35** and **1 Timothy 2:11-12**…"The women are to keep silent in the churches; for they are not permitted to speak, but are to subject themselves, just as the Law also says. If they desire to learn anything, let them ask their own husbands at home; for it is improper for a woman to speak in church" and "A woman must quietly receive instruction with entire submissiveness. But I do not allow a woman to teach or exercise authority over a man, but to remain quiet." We agree with the following statement on the subject: "The uniform testimony of the New Testament is that while women have many valuable ministries, it is not given to them to have public ministry to the whole church. They are entrusted with the unspeakably important work of the home and of raising children. But they are not allowed to speak publicly in the assembly. Theirs is to be a place of submission to the man. It is often contended that what Paul is forbidding in (**1 Corinthians 14:34**) is for the women to chatter or gossip while the service is going on. However, such an interpretation is unsupported. The word here translated 'speak' (laleo) did not mean 'to chatter' in Koin Greek. Indeed, women are not permitted to ask questions publicly in the church. If they want to learn something, they should ask their own husbands at home. Some women might try to evade the previous prohibition against speaking by asking questions. It is possible to teach by the simple act of questioning others. If a woman does not have a husband, she could ask her father, her brother, or one of the elders of the church. This may be translated, 'Let them ask their menfolk at home.'" (MacDonald, William. Believer's Bible Commentary. Nashville: Thomas Nelson Publishers, Inc., 1995).

Although women do not serve as elders, it is evident that they do serve in some capacity, whether individually or in husband/wife partnership, as deacons (diakonos) (**Romans 16:1-4**). Depending on the translation, the word "gune" (**1 Timothy 3:11**) can either mean "woman" or "wife" (the more common translation), allowing the verse to read either "deaconesses" or "wives of the deacons." Either way, the focus is on character and we are given four qualifications particular to women who serve in this capacity. They "must likewise be…" (**1 Timothy 3:11**)

1. **Dignified** (semnós). See #1 for "Qualifications of a Deacon."

2. **Not malicious gossips** (diábolos). Not false accusers or slanderers. **Revelation 12:10** refers to Satan as "the accuser of our brethren." God commands that, "You shall not go about as a slanderer among your people, and you are not to act against the life of your neighbor." **(Leviticus 19:16)** This is less a matter of words than it is a matter of the heart. "But the things that proceed out of the mouth come from the heart, and those defile the man. For out of the heart come evil thoughts, murders, adulteries, fornications, thefts, false witness, slanders. These are the things which defile the man." **(Matthew 15:18-20)** "For we all stumble in many ways. If anyone does not stumble in what he says, he is a perfect man, able to bridle the whole body as well. Now if we put the bits into the horses' mouths so that they will obey us, we direct their entire body as well. Look at the ships also, though they are so great and are driven by strong winds, are still directed by a very small rudder wherever the inclination of the pilot desires. So also the tongue is a small part of the body, and yet it boasts of great things. See how great a forest is set aflame by such a small fire! And the tongue is a fire, the very world of iniquity; the tongue is set among our members as that which defiles the entire body, and sets on fire the course of our life, and is set on fire by hell. For every species of beasts and birds, of reptiles and creatures of the sea, is tamed and has been tamed by the human race. But no one can tame the tongue; it is a restless evil and full of deadly poison. With it we bless our Lord and Father, and with it

we curse men, who have been made in the likeness of God; from the same mouth come both blessing and cursing. My brethren, these things ought not to be this way." **(James 3:2-10)**

3. **Temperate** (nephálios). See #3 for "Qualifications of an Elder."

4. **Faithful in all things** (pistós). Worthy of belief, trust, or confidence. Trust is earned over time. This is similar to #6 for "Qualifications of a Deacon."

Choosing and Equipping Elders and Deacons

We must remember that the Church is a theocracy with Christ at the head. Elders are not elected or voted in by the congregation or by deacons. There are no search committees, resumes, or auditions. Instead, elders are appointed by fellow elders in unanimity, through much prayer, based on the criteria presented in the Bible. The precedent is set by Jesus Himself as we read that, "He went off to the mountain to pray, and He spent the whole night in prayer to God. And when day came, He called His disciples to Him and chose twelve of them, whom He also named as apostles." **(Luke 6:12-13)** As we move forward in the early Church, we see the same example modeled by Paul and Barnabas "when they had appointed elders for them in every church, having prayed with fasting, they commended them to the Lord in whom they had believed." **(Acts 14:23)** Farther on, we see Paul's instruction to

Titus to "set in order what remains and appoint elders in every city." (**Titus 1:5**)

The "laying on of hands by the presbytery" (**1 Timothy 4:14**) is not the imparting of any supernatural gift upon someone. It is simply acknowledging the gift that God has already placed within that person's life. If the elders who are already in place truly meet the Biblical requirements of the role, and if they genuinely understand and appreciate their responsibility in that role, then the unanimous appointing of additional elders should proceed properly. There may still be debate (even heated debate as we see in **Acts 15**), but eventually a unanimous decision should be reached (as we also see in **Acts 15**). This is why it is so important that our elders are committed to prayer for guidance and that our congregation is committed to prayer for our elders. These are important decisions affecting many lives, and these decisions can only be reached when our elders are spiritually in tune with God and with each other.

Scripture does not place a limit on the number of elders in office within a congregation. We see 70 elders of Israel (**Exodus 24, Numbers 11**), 250 chief officers of Solomon (**2 Chronicles 8**), 12 apostles of Jesus (**Luke 6**), an unspecified number of elders of the church in Jerusalem (**Acts 15**), 24 elders around the throne of heaven (**Revelation 4**), etc. A local church may start with only one or two elders. As God grows the congregation, each elder should be diligently praying for and seeking those whom God has raised up to be co-laborers. All elders are equal in authority, serving within a local body together as the presbytery, submitted to the Lord and to one another. Whether in a large congregation or in a small house church, the important thing is that the elders recognize, acknowledge, and embrace the eldership of others within the body of Christ. Since there is no numeric limit to eldership, we should allow and encourage all those whom God has raised up as elders to serve in that capacity. On the other hand, we should not be so quick to try to raise up leaders in our own strength simply to fill a perceived void. If God has not called them, we must not appoint them. The appointing of elders is a serious matter, and we should once again take note of Paul's exhortation to "not lay hands upon anyone too hastily and thereby share responsibility for the sins of others." **(1 Timothy 5:22)** Once an elder is commissioned by the presbytery to go and pastor a separate congregation, the whole cycle repeats itself as other elders emerge within that new local body.

The following diagram shows the general picture of how we should be raising and supporting Church leaders. Note that the structure is not a hierarchy, but rather upholds the equality of eldership within the Church. We spend our time and energy on shepherding rather than on trying to maintain a top-down administrative system. Potential new leaders are found within the congregations themselves. These new leaders are then equipped and commissioned by the elders of those congregations. Some of these new leaders may choose to remain with the original church, while others may be led to start other fellowships (and they will be able to do so knowing that they have the full blessing of their original church family). Multiplying in this way preserves the God-ordained bond between a new pastor, his mentoring elders, and his sending church family.

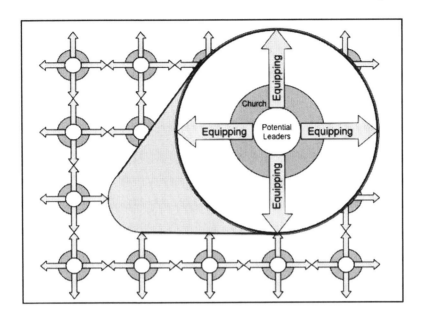

As far as financial support of elders is concerned, we are instructed that, "elders who rule well are to be considered worthy of double honor, especially those who work hard at preaching and teaching. For the Scripture says, 'you shall not muzzle the ox while he is threshing,' and 'The laborer is worthy of his wages.'" **(1 Timothy 5:17-18)** Paul continues this line of thought by saying, "God is not concerned about oxen, is He? Or is He speaking altogether for our sake? Yes, for our sake it was written, because the plowman ought to plow in hope, and the thresher to thresh in hope of sharing the crops. If we sowed spiritual things in you, is it too much if we reap material things from you? If others share the right over you, do we not more? Nevertheless, we did not use this right, but we endure all things so that we will cause no hindrance to the gospel of Christ. Do you not know that those who perform sacred services eat the food of the temple, and those who attend regularly to the altar have their share from the altar? So also the Lord directed those who proclaim the gospel to get their living from the gospel." **(1 Corinthians 9:9-14)**

The term "double honor" has its origin in the inheritance of the first-born son **(Deuteronomy 21:15-17)**, and it clearly speaks of wages. Elders who "rule well" have the right to be supported (generously) by their congregations, "especially those who work hard at preaching and teaching." However, not all elders rule well, and not all elders work hard at preaching and teaching. In addition, not all elders who do rule well avail themselves of this right. Some, like Paul in Corinth, choose not to accept their financial rights so that they would "cause no hindrance to the gospel of Christ." If an elder truly meets the requirements of eldership and does claim the right to just wages, we must consider that our support is appropriately going to a man whose character is "free from the love of money." **(1 Timothy 3:3)** So how much should we pay our elders? This is a tough question, but we believe that a good starting point for a full-time teaching elder is the average salary of the congregation in which he serves. In other words, the sum of everyone's wages divided by the number of wage earners. This approach puts the elder in the same socio-economic position as those whom he serves, allowing him to better relate to the needs of the congregation. If the people are struggling, the pastor is struggling with them; if the people are prosperous, the elder is prosperous as well. Spiritually speaking, there is no difference between paid (staff) elders and unpaid pastors. God's requirements and expectations are the same for both. Our responsibility as a congregation is simply to support our elders through generous giving. We must also take care not to place additional, non-eldership responsibilities upon an elder who does accept payment. The focus of our elders is to concentrate on two things, and two things only: "prayer and the ministry of the word." **(Acts 6:4)** Our financial support is what allows them to do just that.

The process of choosing deacons is very different from that of choosing elders. The selection of deacons, although still theocratic, contains some elements of democracy. In short, deacons are selected from among the congregation, by the congregation, with formal acknowledgement and approval of the elders. Once again, this process is done through much prayer. Our best example is found in the book of Acts at the initiation of the office of deacon. We see that "the twelve summoned the congregation of the disciples and said, 'It is not desirable for us to neglect the word of God in order to serve tables. Therefore, brethren, select from among you seven men of good reputation, full of the Spirit and of wisdom, whom we may put in charge of this task. But we will devote ourselves to prayer and to the ministry of the word.' The statement found approval with the whole congregation; and they chose Stephen, a man full of faith and of the Holy Spirit, and Philip, Prochorus, Nicanor, Timon, Parmenas and Nicolas, a proselyte from Antioch. And these they brought before the apostles; and after praying, they laid their hands on them." **(Acts 6:2-6)** Note that the elders left the selection of deacons up to the congregation, while they themselves remained devoted to "prayer and to the ministry of the word." This is a perfect example of the harmony that should exist within the body of Christ, each member serving in his God-given capacity while trusting the other members to do likewise "until we all attain to the unity of the faith, and of the knowledge of the Son of God, to a mature man, to the measure of the stature which belongs to the fullness of Christ." **(Ephesians 4:13)**

A growing personal walk with Christ is essential for every believer, including (especially) our leaders. "Therefore as you have received Christ Jesus the Lord, so walk in Him, having been firmly rooted and now being built up in Him and established in your faith, just as you were instructed." **(Colossians 2:6-7)** For those of us called to lead, and especially for those of us called to teach, there is often the need to refine our theology or presentation so that we may better serve the body of Christ. The mature Christian life is one that is marked by constant learning and revision. No matter how long or how well we have served, there is always room for improvement. The following is a great example: "A Jew named Apollos, an Alexandrian by birth, an eloquent man, came to Ephesus; and he was mighty in the Scriptures. This man had been instructed in the way of the Lord; and being fervent in spirit, he was speaking and teaching accurately the things concerning Jesus, being acquainted only with the baptism of John; and he began to speak out boldly in the synagogue. But when Priscilla and Aquila heard him, they took him aside and explained to him the way of God more accurately." **(Acts 18:24-26)** Note that Apollos was already teaching the word of God accurately. He just needed some instruction on how to teach it more accurately. Such is often the case with leaders. As Solomon said, "Give instruction to a wise man and he will be still wiser, Teach a righteous man and he will increase his learning." **(Proverbs 9:9)**

For good reason, this chapter concentrated on leadership rather than on the mechanics of our gathering together as the

Church. Our firm belief is that when leadership is managed properly, the rest is managed properly as well, so that "when (we) assemble, each one has a psalm, has a teaching, has a revelation, has a tongue, has an interpretation. Let all things be done for edification. If anyone speaks in a tongue, it should be by two or at the most three, and each in turn, and one must interpret; but if there is no interpreter, he must keep silent in the church; and let him speak to himself and to God. Let two or three prophets speak, and let the others pass judgment. But if a revelation is made to another who is seated, the first one must keep silent. For you can all prophesy one by one, so that all may learn and all may be exhorted; and the spirits of prophets are subject to prophets; for God is not a God of confusion but of peace, as in all the churches of the saints." **(1 Corinthians 14:26-33)**

Regardless of where we serve within the body of Christ, from the pew or the pulpit, the material presented in this book is something that every believer should know and apply. It is time for us to start taking personal responsibility for our own spiritual growth. It is time for us to start being the Church that God has called us to be. Remember…YOU are the Church!

AFTERWORD

I would like to say that people are consistent and logical, but we are not. We claim to believe one thing while our actions prove we believe another. We find ourselves echoing the words of **Mark 9:24**, "Lord, I do believe; help my unbelief!"

Although I have often been accused of being a Bible teacher, my calling has always been to teach others how to study the Bible for themselves. No one needs to hear what I have to say, but we all need to hear what God has to say. And He says it through His Word. Those who know me know that I did not choose to write this book. I was compelled and driven to do so. I would much rather see you read the Bible than read my book written about the Bible, but such are the times in which we live. And that is really the whole point of this book; to direct us back to the Bible, with the hope that we will remain there, for we need nothing more than what God has already written.

For decades, I have watched the Church chase trend after trend, program after program in the hope that somehow some new formula will be the answer, all the while neglecting the answer that God has placed right in front of us in His Word if we would only take the time to read it and put it into practice. The Church does not need a new model. We just need to start practicing the model we have already been given in the way it was intended to be practiced. We need to be the "People of the Book." We need to be the Church.

Steve Lorch
February 17, 2012
Mauldin, South Carolina

Made in the USA
Columbia, SC
05 September 2023